"AN ENORMOUS, IMMENSELY COMPLICATED INTERVENTION":

GROUNDFISH, THE NEW ENGLAND FISHERY MANAGEMENT COUNCIL, AND THE WORLD FISHERIES CRISIS

"AN ENORMOUS, IMMENSELY COMPLICATED INTERVENTION":

GROUNDFISH,
THE NEW ENGLAND FISHERY
MANAGEMENT COUNCIL,
AND THE
WORLD FISHERIES CRISIS

SPENCER APOLLONIO AND JACOB J. DYKSTRA

E-BookTime, LLC
Montgomery, Alabama

"An Enormous, Immensely Complicated Intervention":
Groundfish, the New England Fishery Management Council, and the World Fisheries Crisis

Copyright © 2008 by Spencer Apollonio

Library of Congress Control Number: 2008904579

ISBN: 978-1-59824-833-3

First Edition
Published August 2008
E-BookTime, LLC
6598 Pumpkin Road
Montgomery, AL 36108
www.e-booktime.com

Acknowledgements

This project was undertaken upon the suggestion and urging of our mutual friend Peter Boehmer of Monhegan and Falmouth Foreside, Maine. Chris Kellogg, Deputy Director of the New England Fishery Management Council, Guy Marchessault, formerly Deputy Director of the council, and Charles Yentsch, founder of the Bigelow Laboratory for Ocean Sciences, reviewed and commented on the manuscript. The discussion in September 2004 on the origin of the Magnuson Fishery Conservation and Management Act and the publication of this book were made possible by grants from the Island Foundation, Marion, Massachusetts. The quotation in the title is from *Industry in Trouble* by Margaret Dewar (1983:175). We are grateful for her kind permission to quote extensively from that work. She was a thorough and objective chronicler of the New England Fishery Management Council in its first years. Martha Gleason of Boothbay Harbor, Maine, reviewed the manuscript with an editor's eye. Douglas Bart of Boothbay, Maine, provided essential computer skills. We thank them all most sincerely.

Credits

The authors gratefully acknowledge permission to reproduce portions of the following publications:

Bean, M.J., and M.J. Rowland. 1997. *The Evolution of National Wildlife Law*. Copyright 1997 by The Environmental Defense Fund and World Wildlife Fund-U.S. Westport, CT. Greenwood Publishing Group.

Dobbs, D. 2000. *The Great Gulf: Science and the Struggle to Revive the World's Greatest Fishery*. Washington, D.C. Island Press.

Doeringer, P., P.L. Moss, and D.G. Terkla. 1986. *The New England Fishing Economy: Jobs, Income, and Kinship*. Amherst, MA. University of Massachusetts Press.

Weber, M.I. 2002. *From Abundance to Scarcity: a History of U.S. Marine Fisheries Policy*. Washington, D.C. Island Press.

1) Introduction

The world fisheries crisis

The widely publicized problems and alleged failures of marine fisheries management, especially in New England, have generated much controversy and litigation in recent years. Stocks of fish in the Gulf of Maine and on Georges Bank that once were the wonder of the world were reduced in the 1980s and 1990s to fractions of their former abundance - even to the point of raising concerns about their possible extinctions. Even though it has enjoyed increases in the numbers of several important species since 1995, the New England fishery has been called "the poster-child" (NRC 1999:43) of mismanagement and the New England Fishery Management Council (NEFMC) is considered the villain of the piece. But the problem of effective fisheries management is not confined to New England. Other stocks of fish in the United States are also depleted. The federal government in 2000 declared the west coast groundfish fishery a "disaster." The depletion of stocks and the closures of fisheries in Canada has had major economic repercussions. The United Nations has referred to "the world fisheries crisis." And so this discussion is not just about New England; we believe it has implications for fisheries in general.

If this situation is to be corrected, it is important to understand the reasons for the problems. This book is an inquiry into the causes of fish stock depletions and the difficulties of fisheries management. We do not attempt to account for world-wide failures, but we do have personal knowledge and experience with management in New England from the perspectives of the fisheries and the government. Our discussion is based on that experience. We propose to review various reasons commonly put forth in explanation for the fisheries problems in New England and suggest why, in our view, they do not adequately address the fundamental issues; indeed, we believe they are misleading and counterproductive toward improving fisheries management. We will offer our own views of steps necessary to improve the management of marine fisheries.

Criticisms of the council

We have read several analyses of the New England problems of fisheries management. They offer a spectrum of comments of varying validity, but we have not come across any that, in our opinion, identify *fundamental c*auses of and offer credible arguments for failure. We are persuaded that the problems lie deeper than suggested in any of these critiques. And we believe that even if the criticisms and alleged reasons for failure in New England had some validity, it is highly unlikely that they could explain failures in fisheries under very different management regimes, as in Canada for example. Indeed, senior scientists of the National Marine Fisheries Service (NMFS) (Sissenwine and Rosenberg 1993) wrote:

> Although blaming the Magnuson Act [the governing fish-
> eries legislation] for the problems of U.S. fisheries may be
> tempting, the issues are far more complex. First, scientists
> should recognize that problems facing U.S. fisheries are
> common throughout the world. This is not an excuse, but it
> does imply that a legal framework for fisheries manage-
> ment unique to the United States is not the underlying
> cause of the problem.

These authors offer three components - limited entry, rapid expansion of scientific information, and "risk-averse" management decisions - for a solution to the problem. Our discussion here will suggest that these would be insufficient remedies.

A few examples will suffice to illustrate our concerns about common criticisms. One review (Shelley et al. 1996:222) asks "have all the lessons that should be learned from the 'New England situation' been recognized?" Those authors suggest that "the problems....are institutional and structural failures that may lie far more deeply than the legislative reach of the FCMA [the Magnuson Act]." Further, Shelley and his colleagues (1996:233) note that "the problems... raise more fundamental questions [beyond 'legislative remedies'] about the factors that determine economically and ecologically healthy fisheries." They ask "whether current efforts to tighten the existing regulatory framework will in fact improve New England's ability to manage for both ecological and economic sustainability." They note (p 233) that some of the problems "seem to go beyond legislative remedies." And, they add (p 239): "It is now clear to us that long-term solutions will require a much deeper and more persistent effort that addresses the entire complex of factors that define the success of a managed fishery." We like their questions and believe their observation about deeper and more persistent effort is appropriate - it is the same position that we take here - and their suggestions are insightful, particularly in view of repeated calls to amend and amend the Magnuson Fishery Conservation and Management Act (MFCMA). [1] Nevertheless, of those authors' five recommendations, three depend explicitly upon legislative action, and one probably would require legislative action, or at least administrative interpretation of MFCMA. The fifth recommendation has to do with more practices and more information of the traditional kind common in fisheries management today on which to base management plans and action. In other words, Shelley and his co-authors recommend more of the same - adequate information, administration, enforcement, compliance, and evaluation. We do

---

[1] The original legislation was named in honor of Senator Warren G. Magnuson of Washington, a principal sponsor of the act. MFCMA has more recently been known as the Magnuson-Stevens Fisheries Management Act, referring to Senator Ted Stevens of Alaska, a sponsor of later amendments. The MFCMA was substantially amended in 1996 by the Sustainable Fisheries Act (SFA). We will continue to refer to it here as MFCMA as it was known during our tenures with the New England council.

not disagree with the necessity for these components of an effective plan, but we do not see that these recommendations address fundamental questions or probe far more deeply than common concerns about MFCMA itself. We are disappointed that this analysis did not produce the fundamental insights that it advocated as necessary.

The Boston Globe on October 26, 2003, began a four-part series of reports on the New England fisheries. It asserted that the New England Fisheries Management Council [2] "refused to set limits that are strict enough" to prevent stock depletions, and that the council "dithered" in the face of the crisis. The *Globe*'s first assertion is factually wrong. Within our experience with the council, in its first ten years, it set very strict limits - and then repeatedly found that the limits did little or nothing to control or restrain fish mortalities; indeed, there was evidence that the strict limits exacerbated the problem of excessive fish mortalities. The *Globe* series, in fact, begins in dramatic fashion with an example of this reality; the first story in the series described fishermen throwing overboard - unavoidably killing and wasting - fish that were illegal under the existing regulations. We will consider why such stringent limits did not work and suggest lessons to be learned from that failure. And we disagree with the second *Globe* assertion that the council during our terms "dithered." (The

---

[2] The New England Fishery Management Council is responsible for preparation of management plans for the marine fisheries off New England. It is a "quasi-federal" agency composed of seventeen voting members and four non-voting members. Eleven of the voting members are nominated by governors of the five coastal New England states and appointed by the Secretary of Commerce. Five are the principal fisheries officers of each state and one is the Regional Administrator of the National Marine Fisheries Service. The non-voting members are representatives of the Department of State, the United States Coast Guard, the United States Fish and Wildlife Service, and the Atlantic States Marine Fisheries Commission. All serve on the council on a part-time basis. The council has a small full-time scientific and administrative staff.

Portland [Maine] *Press Herald* repeated the charge of "dithering" in November 2005.) To the contrary, our experience was that the council tried very hard in those ten years, as we shall describe, to develop a management plan that would conserve fish without shutting down the fishing industry. We do not consider that many council committee meetings and the serious and intense full council discussions, even until late at night and all trying to correct serious problems, can be characterized as "dithering." There was no time in that first ten years in which the council was not trying by any practical means to constrain the catch within the quotas, or Optimum Yields (OYs), recommended by fisheries scientists and without shutting down the New England fishing industry.

Carl Safina (1997:31) remarked that

the council allowed the free fall of New England populations of cod, haddock, flounder, and other important species, sending them to their lowest levels in history.... year after year, the New England Fishery Management Council never got its act together, despite continual controversy and withering hand-wringing. [Safina stated that the MFCMA] appointed those most knowledgeable about the fisheries - people who fish - to be responsible for regulating fishing activities.[3] But the council system's uniquely idealized form of representative self-government did not work as intended, because people with financial stakes in the outcomes of their own self-regulation do not always act ideally. Putting billions of dollars' worth of fish in front of the industry and asking them to police themselves was not terribly realistic....The councils made hardly a move to restore, conserve or even regulate.

This latter allegation is hardly supported by the record of stringent quotas imposed in 1977 and later years, and before Safina's book was published the council had again imposed increasingly stringent limits on the groundfish fleet. Safina makes no mention

---

[3] Should MFCMA appoint people not knowledgeable about fisheries?

of what, in his view, the council should have done.

A most common charge against the council system in general and the New England council in particular is that

> the foxes are guarding the henhouse. Councils are domin-
> ated by fishing representatives who often act in their short-
> term interests instead of in the long-term interest of the
> nation and of the fish... the New England Fishery Manage-
> ment Council had become perhaps the most notorious of
> our nation's eight such councils (Fordham 1996:129-130).

A number of critics of the New England council repeat the assertion that it is dominated by self-serving fisheries represent- atives with obvious conflicts of interest. *The Christian Science Monitor* (Dec. 18, 2003:17) featured this criticism. The *Globe* series referred to earlier also made this charge. The *Globe* also noted, with apparent inconsistency, that of seventeen voting members of the New England council just six (roughly one industry representative from each of the five coastal states) were members of the commercial fishing industry. A book on the New England fisheries (Carey 1999:301) stated "They... got substantial industry representation on the eight regional... councils.... Certain of the seats would go to environmentalists, academics, and consumer advocates, but there were enough seats to make industry *control of* the regional councils a probability" (emphasis added).

Michael Weber (2002), who had served four years as a special assistant to the chief of the National Marine Fisheries Service, wrote a very informative history of the marine fisheries policies of the United States and their administration by NMFS and its predecessor agencies. He was quite critical of the performance of the New England council. Weber (2202:200) asserted that the membership of the councils in general were dominated by fishermen. Colin Woodward (2004:224) also declared that representatives from the groundfishing industry dominated the New England council. The number of "industry" representatives on the New England council from 1977 to 1986 averaged just six; only in 1982 were there seven industry representatives on the council. The assertions that five or six or even seven industry representatives could "dominate" or "control" the council implies that the other eleven or twelve voting members, including five state fisheries directors and the Regional Administrator of NMFS, were incapable of thinking and voting their own minds.

Even if industry representatives had ever voted as a solid block (which, in our experience, they rarely did on pivotal management questions), they would have always been in a minority. Nor is it the case that they always voted out of self-interest. The charge that the council is dominated by self-serving, interest-conflicted members is hardly credible, as the council's voting records show.

Richard Ellis (2003:69) wrote that MFCMA "left planning and quotas to 'regional councils,' which meant that every fishing community could set its own limits - a classic example of the fox guarding the henhouse." This statement is of course factually wrong; this sort of misinformation is a disservice to MFCMA, to the council, and to all those seriously concerned with solving the problems of fisheries management. The obscenities and threats of violence directed by fishermen at council members as they voted for very strict regulations in December 1997 (*Commercial Fisheries News* (CFN) January 1998:8A) are hardly consistent with a picture of a community setting its own limits or with Ellis's statement.

While noting the "fox-in-the-hen-house" view, David Dobbs (2000:58) took a broader view of the problem:

Such self-interested resistance [by the fishing industry] to regulation... definitely has played and still plays a role in the failure of most councils to restrain fishing. However, the system failed also for the simple reason that these clumsy, rather slow-footed regulatory bodies found themselves overwhelmed, underarmed, and frequently confused by the rapidly deteriorating situations they faced in the

1980s and 1990s.

Almost from their beginnings the councils faced a fast-blooming crisis that demanded quick action. Along with rapidly accelerating rates of overfishing (which were partly due to the incentives created and strengthened by Magnuson [i. e., MFCMA] and the debt-driven expansion of the 1980s), their challenges included the complicated, decentralized nature of both fishery ecology and the fishing industry; the extreme difficulty of predicting the effects of any given management measure; a tool bag, put together by precedent and Congressional action, that offered mostly unwieldy or ineffective regulatory measures; and the doubt, in the face of large catches and seemingly abundant fish, that many fishermen held about NMFS's warnings of population decline. It didn't help that the councils met only about a dozen times a year. [4]

Although Dobbs's observation is more realistic, we find that it also misses more fundamental problems in our approaches to fisheries management.

Industry representatives are included in the council for the obvious reason that their special expertise is needed when considering the "extraordinarily diverse" (Shelley et al. 1996:223) and complex fisheries – *all* the fisheries, not just groundfish - off New England. MFCMA specifies that eleven voting members "must be individuals who, by reason of their occupational or other experience, scientific expertise, or training, are knowledgeable regarding the conservation and management, or the commercial or

---

[4] NEFMC's groundfish committee met considerably more then a dozen times a year. In one two-year period it met more than forty times. Council members also participated in other species committee meetings during the year. It was in such committee meetings that the problems and details of management plans were worked out. Council members took part in those committee meetings in addition to the regular full council meetings.

recreational harvest, of the fishery resources of the geographical area concerned." [5] The groundfishery of Maine is not the same as that of Chatham, Massachusetts, or Point Judith, Rhode Island. The groundfisheries of Gloucester differed significantly from those of Boston and New Bedford. The same is true of the lobster, scallop, and herring fisheries. Six fishing representatives out of seventeen voting members does not seem to be an unreasonable or excessive number to provide that special and essential knowledge for effective management of all the New England marine fisheries that is required by law.

Finally, a state fishery management agency of New England, recommending changes to mitigate groundfisheries problems, recently identified the need to "build more flexibility and balance into the Sustainable Fisheries Act [i e, MFCMA] "as the "long-term root cause of the problem." The agency did not define "flexibility" or "balance", but however defined we do not find much promise in the incorporation of such subjective and nebulous concepts into the act. Surely something more specific than such vague terms, open to many possible interpretations or definitions, is needed. We do not believe, in fact, that amendments by themselves to the fisheries management act can solve underlying and fundamental problems. We do not believe that any deficiencies of the original MFCMA itself could be considered "root causes" of the problem, particularly when the failures of fisheries management are found not just in fisheries under the jurisdiction of the New England council or the United States but also throughout the world in fisheries not subject to MFCMA.

We could cite other published explanations of the fisheries problems, all, in our opinion, of equally dubious validity. Critics of the council or of our effort here may reply that all these examples are just "straw men" raised to apologize for or exculpate the New England council and to avoid the *real* cause for management failure - that the council refused to get tough, to "bite the bullet," and to apply meaningful species catch quotas

---

[5] MFCMA, Sec. 302(b)(2)(A).

and implement limited entry of one kind or another. Such measures, critics of the council and of our analysis may assert, would *really* control fishing effort and fishing mortality and thus lead to stock restorations and sustainability. We shall not avoid these issues; we shall consider them in detail. The council of course did implement strict catch-and-landings quotas as its first act and tried to maintain and enforce them for close to five years in spite of serious problems injurious to the fish stocks arising directly from the quotas. And there are substantive reasons why the council in our experience did not invoke measures for some form of limited entry even though that idea was considered at length. Quotas and limited entry are not simple and straight-forward management measures that would guarantee stock restorations and lead to effective management for sustainable fisheries. But they warrant and will require more consideration than is appropriate at this point in our review of the council.

In reviewing this history and analysis of the council management of fisheries, it should be kept in mind that while our concern here is exclusively with groundfish, the part-time council assisted by a staff of four scientists was simultaneously concerned, as required by MFCMA, with development of management plans for a number of species - herring, scallops, squid, and others - each of which was contentious and had its own particular problems. Council members served on committees for the preparation of plans for each of those species, meeting separately from the regular council meetings. The council members also served on a number of committees concerned with ancillary matters such as council finances and administration, enforcement, environmental matters, foreign fishing, and gear conflicts; thus the seventeen voting council members, all serving on a part-time basis, were never able to focus exclusively on the problems of a single fishery. By any measure, the council was spread thin.

The perspective of the authors

This discussion is based upon our experiences with the first ten years of the management council. Much has happened in the twenty years since we served, but we believe that the essential and fundamental problems were encountered and confronted in those early years, and we believe that the reasons for what has continued since those years to be difficult and contentious can be found in that ten-year period.

We came to this experience and to this discussion with quite different backgrounds. Dykstra has over sixty years of personal fisheries experience at all levels - at sea on fishing vessels; with politicians, managers, and scientists at state, regional, federal and international levels; as a founder and president of a fishermen's cooperative; as a member of the U.S. delegation to Law of the Sea Conferences of the United Nations, as a prime mover in the creation of the 200-mile limit and MFCMA; and as a council member for seven years. He was chairman of the council during his last year with the council. Apollonio is a marine biologist who has carried on basic marine biological and applied fisheries research; administered a state fisheries management agency for over ten years; was the first executive director, for two years, of NEFMC; and was a voting member of the council for eight years, a total of ten years with the council and twenty years in fisheries science and management. In spite of our different histories and perspectives prior to and during our service with the council, we have a perhaps surprising degree of agreement on the nature of the problems. This is the background and perspective from which the observations and opinions in this book are derived.

2) Encountering Reality - The Cod Crisis of 1977

The New England groundfish industry in 1977

Congress in 1976 enacted legislation, the Magnuson Fishery Conservation and Management Act, that created an exclusive Fisheries Conservation Zone (FCZ) [6] from three miles out to 200 miles from our shores for the purpose of removing heavy foreign fishing, which had greatly reduced fish stocks, from U.S. coastal waters. The legislation also established a new national policy for 1) the *development* of domestic fisheries and 2) the management of domestic fisheries within the FCZ in the best interests of the nation. It created eight regional fisheries management councils to implement that policy; the job of the council is the development and implementation of fisheries management plans (FMPs) to attain the purposes of MFCMA.

The New England fishing industry had been a principal advocate of the legislation, but it paid greatest attention to the part that excluded foreign fishing within the 200-mile zone, and it paid little attention to the mandate for management of the domestic fisheries. In an comprehensive review of the problems of the New England fisheries since the World War Two, Margaret Dewar (1983:147, 149) described the mood in the fishing industry as the New England Fishery Management Council began its work:

> As Congress passed the 200-mile limit legislation, the New England groundfish industry saw a brighter future than ever before. Once the foreigners were excluded, those in

---

[6] FCZ is now known as the Exclusive Economic Zone (EEZ).

the industry felt more confident about the maintenance of the fish stocks. In contrast to the foreigners, New England fishermen, they pointed out, used larger mesh, lacked technology for midwater trawling, and did not have the capacity which caused the damage to the stocks. Recovery of the groundfish stocks became possible, and, with that, the industry's prosperity seemed likely to last. In larger numbers than ever before, fishermen and boat owners planned to build and buy new boats, and young people decided fishing offered a promising career. The 200-mile limit, fishermen, boat owners, and processors felt, had solved the most important problems the industry faced, and they looked optimistically toward the next years.... Hundreds of fishermen in Gloucester, Portland, and smaller Maine and Massachusetts ports decided to purchase new boats.

The groundfish plan of 1977

The New England Fishery Management Council officially became active in January of 1977. A month before, at one of several preliminary organizational meetings, it was handed a management plan for codfish, haddock, and yellowtail flounder, species considered to be at risk, prepared by NMFS at an earlier request of the council. The council at that time had no staff to either prepare a management plan or to review and critique the NMFS plan on behalf of the council.

The council itself had little opportunity to consider or debate the plan; the Regional Administrator of NMFS insisted that the council implement the plan as rapidly as possible - immediately, in fact - because of a presumed looming resource crisis within the fisheries. There was a sense of urgency because the existing management regulations under the International Commission for Northwest Atlantic Fisheries (ICNAF), which had had management authority in the region since 1950, expired in December 1976 and MFCMA did not officially become operative until March 1977. In the two-month interim, it was feared, there would be an unregulated fishery with the possibility of excessive removals of fish by American fishermen from depleted stocks. "NMFS officials pressed the Council to adopt a plan without the opportunity to understand or debate the NMFS draft" (Dewar 1983:156). The sense of urgency was such that the Regional Administrator of NMFS had sent the plan to Washington for approval *before* the council itself had had an opportunity for review, comment, or approval, the reverse of the proper procedure. This may have reflected a view within NMFS that the council was not a substantive player in the process.

The plan prepared by NMFS was essentially quite simple. After describing the depleted condition of fish stocks, it proposed certain specified tonnages as annual landings quotas for the three species considered to be in greatest danger of further depletion. The quotas were:

codfish	30,000 mt
haddock	6,200 mt, as a bycatch only
yellowtail flounder	14,800 mt

The quotas were based upon old ICNAF records which, as it turned out, were unreliable (Hennessey and Healey 2000:195). But, wrote Margaret Dewar (1983:156),

> The management measures offered little basis for optimism about the results of fishery management during the years to follow. The regulations came directly from ICNAF; even the numbers of pounds allowed as bycatch were the same. The ICNAF experience should have suggested good reasons to try other methods because ICNAF had failed to regulate the use of the fish stocks. Perhaps the Council attributed ICNAF's failure to the intractability of the foreigners rather than to flaws in the management approaches themselves. Perhaps NMFS did not have the power to propose new measures when Council members might more readily accept old ones already debated many times. Neither the Council nor NMFS had enough time or

knowledge to attempt new approaches.

The cod quota was lowered to 25,000 mt in the final regulations of June 1977. Note that the haddock quota was for bycatch only. Bycatch refers to those fish taken incidental to the capture of target species. (The term "incidental catch" is now occasionally used in place of bycatch.) The intent was that there should be no directed target fishery for haddock because of its severely depleted condition. Ideally, no haddock should be taken at all. But some haddock would inevitably and unavoidably be taken incidental to fishing for cod or other groundfish species such as pollock, flounders, or hakes, most of which were not considered to be seriously depleted. If there were to be any fishery at all for those species, then some provision had to be made for the bycatch of haddock. If no haddock at all could be taken, then there could be no significant groundfish fishery in New England.

The plan proposed that when those tonnages were landed the directed fisheries for those species would be closed for the rest of the year. The vessels would then be permitted to land no more than rather small "trip limits" to accommodate the bycatch of regulated species unavoidably taken in other fisheries.

The plan also proposed that certain areas be closed to otter trawling - the principal method of taking groundfish - to protect spawning fish which tend to congregate in generally known areas, and it proposed minimum mesh sizes in the otter trawl nets to permit immature fish to escape through the meshes of the nets. It also specified minimum sizes of fish that could be landed, also to protect immature fish. Finally, it proposed a limit of the pounds of yellowtail flounder that could be landed for each fisherman on board a vessel, with a maximum number of 30,000 pounds for each vessel per trip.

In short, the plan proposed:

- annual quotas for three species
- closed areas

- mesh sizes
- minimum fish sizes
- landings limits per trip

The plan contained little or no consideration or analyses of possible biological, economic, political, or social consequences of the proposed quotas, trip limits, or closures. The plan in its one-paragraph consideration of possible economic impacts stated that "the proposed regulatory measures should impose no substantial adverse impacts." The plan went on to state that "stricter conservation measures could be implemented, but would cause severe hardships to the industry." NMFS apparently believed that the proposed quotas and other measures would lead to stock restorations and with no adverse impacts upon the fishing industry. If these statements now seem naive in view of what was to follow, it should be understood that fisheries management of this kind was an entirely new endeavor in the United States; no one - neither NMFS nor the newly-appointed members of the council - had had any experience with fisheries management on this scale. Weber (2002:78) noted that "Until the passage of the Magnuson-Stevens Act, the [salmon] fisheries in Alaska remained the principal source of experience in marine fisheries management for federal agencies. Otherwise, the role of federal fisheries agencies in fisheries management had remained advisory." The MFCMA was in fact an experiment with very little prior experience to guide it. but it should be noted here, as David Pierce (MS 1982:9), a long-time council member, noted, "Scientists' advice was respected and heeded by the Council."

Margaret Dewar (1983:154-5) described the plan as

> an odd document. The plan specified no goals, although a major implicit purpose... was that the management of the fishery resources should aim to rebuild or stabilize the fish stocks....The Council agreed on this purpose... partly because the plan only defined some aspects of the goal. The lack of definition allowed each member to form his own impression of what the goal meant. The plan

mentioned 'undue economic impacts'... and 'adverse economic impacts'... but never said what these were....The plan did not demonstrate that the [management] measures selected would achieve the purposes. Such analyses would have been nearly impossible, however, as long as the goals remained so vague.

David Pierce (MS 1982:8) also noted:

A significant part of these final regulations - which didn't seem too important at the time - was the stipulation that the Regional Director [of NMFS] was to close fisheries; i.e., was to stop the taking of *any* cod, haddock, or yellowtail flounder when total catch of any of the species - with allowance for expected bycatch for the rest of the year - equaled 100% of the quota. This decision effectively made it mandatory for the Regional Director to close. He and the Council had no flexibility to take any other action regardless of the economic consequence to the industry or any sort of extenuating circumstance.

And Margaret Dewar (1983:155) wrote:

Furthermore... the biological assessments of stock conditions and the schedule for rebuilding, did not receive sufficient Council discussion and agreement. The biologists' presentation of data to the Council gave the impression of more confidence in the figures than the scientists themselves felt. The biologists knew that stock assessments had a wide margin of error particularly for recent year classes and that the relation between spawning stock size and size of a new year class was virtually unknown.

At its January 1977 meeting the council directed its newly-hired executive director to take the plan to the required public hearings preparatory to implementing the plan with emergency regulations as soon as possible. The hearings required by MFCMA were duly held, and the council then convened in late February to consider the public comments and its course of action. During the course of the somewhat perfunctory council discussion, the question was asked, "What happens if the tonnages are in fact reached within the year and closures are implemented?" The only response to this question from NMFS or the council was that because the stocks were reputed to be so low, the fishing industry could not possibly catch that many fish. [7] And so the plan was unanimously approved and implemented on an emergency basis because of the perceived urgency of immediate action to prevent stock collapses.

This first groundfish plan was quite simple, but its implications and consequences were not. In hindsight it is clear that the council should have asserted its authority for plan preparation, and taken its time to give careful scrutiny, as it soon learned to do, to the probable consequences of the plan, some of which could have been anticipated even then and in the absence of the experience that was to follow.

The first surprise

But then a totally unexpected thing happened.

> Landings in the early part of 1977 seemed to be supportive of many fishermen's claims that cod were everywhere, and they couldn't be avoided. During the first four months of 1977, "Codfish landings throughout New England were nearly twice what they were the previous spring (13.4 million pounds compared to 7.3 million pounds)... Piers in Gloucester and New Bedford were groaning under the load of spring landings and there was much concern that processing houses for frozen fish were going to be grossly inadequate. Processors were running their facilities seven

---

[7] This response obviously ignored the implication that if the stocks were indeed that low, then why had NMFS suggested such relatively high quotas? But at the time, the council was so inexperienced and the sense of urgency and haste were such that it was easy to overlook such subtleties.

days a week in June and adding extra shifts, and still they could not keep up with the boats" (Pierce MS 1982:13). [8]

The apparent abundance of fish began to raise questions in the minds of the council members as to the accuracy of the scientific stock assessments.

By May, less than three months after the plan was implemented, it was clear that the council faced the first crisis of many in its history. NMFS advised the council that at the current rate of fishing the cod quota for the Gulf of Maine for *all* of the year 1977 would be taken by the end of June. [9] For the first time, and like a sledge-hammer blow, it became apparent that the council had to face the consequences of an extended shutdown of the entire New England groundfishing industry. An industry shutdown, it suddenly became apparent, was unavoidable if the quota was to be enforced because of the unavoidable bycatch of codfish in the otter trawl fisheries for other species of the region. No matter what the target species - hakes or flounders or pollock - some cod would be taken, and the accumulated bycatch of cod in those other fisheries could be substantial.

Since fishermen could not avoid catching these species when fishing for other groundfish or flounder, they had to stop fishing altogether. Fishermen, boat owners, and dealers had never experienced such an order. Indeed a measure that ordered people to stop working but offered them no compensation was extremely unusual for workers in any industry....The government was preventing fishermen from working, not offering incentives not to work, but offering nothing in return (Dewar 1983:167).

---

[8] The quotation is from *National Fisherman,* August 1977:3A, 40A.

[9] Reported groundfish landings by U.S. fishermen increased by thirty-four percent in 1977.

Unanticipated consequences

A closure of fishing could also mean the shutdown of processing plants and lay-offs of plant workers; shutdowns of suppliers of fishing gear, fuel, and maintenance and repair services, and of distribution and marketing chains of fish products. A closure for perhaps six months - for the rest of the year 1977 - would suspend or drastically reduce the activities of an industry worth hundreds of millions of dollars to the New England economy. There were those who argued that the industry as a whole could not survive such a closure; the essential supportive infrastructure would surely be lost. Or the processing sector of the industry would be forced to import fish from other countries to maintain its marketing shares and structure; to do otherwise would mean that their markets could not be retained or recovered when domestic fish might again be available at some uncertain date in the future. The prospect of catching the cod quota by June brought home to the council the wide-spread and substantial consequences of its hasty and rather casual action of plan approval without serious consideration or discussion in February. The council then began to realize that fisheries management would not be easy. In this context, we recall some naiveté evident very early in this first-ever experiment with fisheries management, before the council actually began operations. There were those who questioned what there would be for the council to do once it had implemented management plans. How would the council manage to keep busy once plans were in effect and, presumably, leading inevitably to stock restoration and maintenance? Would the council be dissolved or put on a stand-by basis? How could it justify its existence?

NMFS closed the directed fishery for cod for the Gulf of Maine on July 7. Only small bycatch takings - trip limits - of cod would be permitted after that date for the rest of the year. In addition, NMFS notified the council that eighty percent of the haddock and yellowtail flounder quotas would be taken by July 15, and the cod quota on Georges Bank would be taken by August 17. The problem on Georges Bank was exacerbated by a reduction of the cod quota there from 20,000 mt to 16,650 mt. This was necessary under the U.S.-Canadian Reciprocal Fisheries Agreement that recognized the traditional Canadian fisheries on the bank and was signed into law by the president on July 26, 1977. NMFS closed the U.S. fishery on Georges Bank on August 16. Contrary to NMFS's pollyannaish economic impact analysis of the proposed regulations in January, by September 1977 it was very clear that there would be severe economic hardship to the industry.

Within four months of the implementation of the plan that was to last for the full year, and less than six months into its first year the council was faced with a major crisis, the likely disruption of the multi-million-dollar fishing industry.

3) The Objective of the Book

An unending controversy

Thirty years have come and gone since MFCMA was enacted and NEFMC assumed responsibility for management of the marine fisheries off New England. Throughout most of that considerable time the council has been reacting to crises and increasing litigation and threats of litigation. It has been the target of continuing criticisms [10] and the focus of unending controversies. Although there have been encouraging increases recently in the biomasses of some fish species under its jurisdiction, possibly because of its stringent regulations, very little has gone well for the council in that time, and there are few if any indications that the history and climate of turmoil and crisis management and ongoing litigation are likely to change.

One must ask why for all those years has this unhappy situation persisted? Why has the level of controversy and criticism of the council and fisheries management increased, as it undoubtedly has, even with evidence of increasing stock sizes - criticisms from all sides, from the fishing industry and from conservationists and environmentalists? Why has the council apparently failed to respond to wide-spread criticism, especially from conservation groups, that it should enact ever-more stringent regulations to protect and rebuild stocks of fish? What has been learned from allegedly failed efforts to manage or restore fish stocks and from dissension and recriminations and litigations over the means and the ends of those efforts? One suspects that indeed little if

---

[10] See Playfair, S.R., 2003, as an example of a recent, book-length criticism of the council.

anything has been learned, for several reasons:

1) There are numerous proposed amendments to MFCMA at each period of re-authorization, suggesting that there is continuing hope that a revision or change in the law here or there will somehow improve the situation (we expect further amendments in the next re-authorization cycle).

2) Legal challenges of various kinds seem now to be driving the management process. (NMFS is challenged nationwide by more than 140 law suits (Alverson 2002:14)). Indeed, the court has been a large presence in recent management of New England groundfish.

3) Management plans are of ever-increasing complexity (Amendment 13 to the New England Groundfish plan in 2003 is over 1600 pages long; this in part is because of the regulatory review process). The plans are increasingly costly for monitoring, enforcement, and compliance, and render the entire concept of management confusing, or of questionable effectiveness, and of ever decreasing credibility.

None of these are indications of progress or of improvement in the basic concept or process of fisheries management, and none of them suggest or imply any significant long-term benefit for the fish stocks; if anything, they suggest a process in disarray. [11] There are those, of course, who will disagree with this opinion because of the recent increases in some stock numbers, but they cannot dispute the reality of the three characteristics just listed of prevailing fisheries management. They suggest a stumbling, or at worst a failed, experiment in public policy formulation. And so the critical question is why is it so apparently flawed?

---

[11] One person well acquainted for many years with the council does not agree that the process is in disarray. He does think there are serious problems and "it amazes me that it [the council] can function at all. It seems to be lurching forward, but I don't think it is as responsive as it needs to be to changing circumstances in the fishery. Decision making and approval are much too slow."

We participated for the first ten years of this experiment, and we have viewed the subsequent years with growing conviction that fundamental revisions are necessary - but not of the kind proposed by amendments to MFCMA, most of which appear to be merely fine-tuning and of questionable relevance to basic problems. There appears to be little public discussion or debate about whether *fundamental* changes are necessary or what their character might be. Indeed, our impression is that the situation will continue to be fraught with law suits, ever-increasing complexities, and controversies over the purposes of management, and all of questionable benefit to the fish stocks or the fishing industry.

Learning from history

We intend here to review the history of the council in its first ten years with the purpose of examining what it did and did not do and why. We intend to review the consequences to the fish resource of those actions, and to draw what lessons we can from that review. This effort will be based upon our personal experiences with the council, but we shall not rely solely upon our fallible memories. Our review will be supported by the documentation of contemporary records. Further, we shall review, from the written record, the history of the council since 1986, with the intent of comparing the actions and results of recent years with those of the earlier years. We hope that this comparative review will facilitate the identification of the lessons necessary for real improvement in the management process.

Unproductive criticisms

If critics of the council persist in advocating peripheral or false explanations for the problems, as many of them do, that will only distract attention from fundamental issues that we believe underlie the continuing problems and failures - and we do acknowledge the failures in our time with the council. We prefer to attempt instead to develop a recognition and understanding of what, in our opinion, are fundamental problems in fisheries management that to date have not been recognized or adequately analyzed. We do this because we are persuaded that if these issues are not recognized, acknowledged, and addressed, then fisheries management will continue to at best stumble. If the issues that we will suggest are basic and essential to good management are not addressed, we believe that management of fisheries as complex as those of the New England groundfishery cannot succeed. (Presciently, fisheries scientist Peter Larkin observed: "The consequences of harvesting mixed species continue to haunt us like a can of many kinds of worms" ((Larkin 1972:190)). We are persuaded that more amendments to the MFCMA, or more data, or stricter limits of the usual kind, or different administrative regimes or management authorities, or tougher enforcement will not help - that none of these by themselves or collectively can solve the problem - unless fundamental problems are corrected. Management can only succeed by identification and rectification of the problems that have prevented success to date.

Fundamental problems

After reviewing the problems the council encountered in its first ten years and later, we will try to identify the essential lessons. We do not attempt to provide analysis and answers to all the myriad issues that came up within our experience with the council. But we can document enough examples of tactics that did not work to suggest the necessity to question traditional assumptions underlying fishery management. And we believe we can identify certain basic issues, common to all multispecies groundfisheries wherever they are pursued and regardless of the nature of the prevailing management regime, that must be addressed. These issues, we believe, are essential to effective groundfish management, regardless of a definition of Optimum Yield, or of the management objective mandated by MFCMA, or of whatever objectives are chosen as the basis of a management plan. These, to anticipate our conclusions, focus on:

1) *benign* and *selective* fishing technologies;

2) truly effective methods for control of fishing effort or, more properly, of fishing mortality; and

3) understanding of the structure and functions of fisheries ecosystems.

These are fundamental and closely interconnected issues. There is ongoing discussion about each of these issues, of course, but none of these, in our opinion, are being addressed in such a way as to suggest significant improvements in management. A principal goal of this effort is to make clear why attention to and innovation in these three areas is essential for effective fisheries management. We are in fact calling for a complete re-thinking of management objectives, management processes, and management tactics if there is to be progress in the restoration and conservation of fisheries as diverse and dynamic as those off New England.

4) The Council History 1977-1986... and Beyond [12]

Reacting to crisis

The first council reaction to the groundfish closures of July and August 1977 was that because of all the adverse implications and ramifications, an industry-wide shutdown was not acceptable. But this was not a unanimous council reaction; some members were ready to let the chips fall where they might. The majority of the council searched rather desperately for a way out of the looming disaster. Within all that activity, discussion, and debate there was no apparent recognition and certainly no discussion that a shutdown - a closure - of a fishery is not a legitimate management tactic but is in fact a symptom or acknowledgement of failure of *management*. The termination of fishing is not management of fishing. The idea of fisheries closures of the kind facing the New England industry is akin to the notion that villages in war must be destroyed in order to save them. In this case the villages are those of fishing families trying to follow centuries-old traditional ways of life.

A number of proposals to avoid closures were brought forth, most from within the council itself. One of them was to deduct the overrun of the quota in 1977, whatever that might be, from the 1978 quota. It would in fact let the fishing continue for the rest of the year, but with payment, on inevitably harsher terms of course, to be made in the following year. Another proposal was to slow

---

[12] A useful history of fisheries management in New England, 1977-1999, was prepared by Hennessey and Healey (2002), and with some interpretations that differ from ours.

the intended rate of stock rebuilding; that is, instead of rebuilding
the three stocks in five years as the NMFS plan recommended,
adjust the quotas to achieve a more gradual stock restoration in
ten years. After all, it was argued, a five-year rebuilding schedule
was an arbitrary decision. If restoration could be attained in ten
years with less pain and disruption, that was a better plan. The
council, in fact, asked NMFS scientists whether larger quotas with
slower stock rebuilding rates would be injurious to the stocks.
The scientists in effect answered "No." And in a court case at
about that time, the judge ruled that there was "nothing in the Act
which prescribes a particular annual rate at which a below-par
stock need be rebuilt" (Bean and Rowland 1997:173). Another
proposal, suggested in December 1977, was to divide the year
into quarters, each with its quota, so that if there had to be closed
periods they would be for relatively brief periods, and spread
throughout the year, such that they would not have the dire
consequences that a six-months shut-down would create. The
presentation and discussion of the various proposals, and their
consequences, proceeded through a number of emergency groundfish committee and full council meetings. Committee discussions
often continued until late at night. The council looked desperately
for a solution. It would continue to look for solutions for the next
five years.

The rise and fall of industry euphoria

Over 180 fishermen attended the council meeting in September
1977. Suddenly the full implications of MFCMA had caught the
attention of the industry. Until then it had largely assumed that
MFCMA had been for the purpose of eliminating foreign fishing
from U.S. waters. The management mandates of the law had been
largely overlooked or ignored in the euphoria of excluding
foreign fishing vessels that were seen to be the real threat to the
industry.

The whole New England fishing industry had suffered in the
depression of the 1930s. There had been a few years of greater
incomes during the later years of World War Two, but then there

was another decline after 1950.

> Although everyone did not share in the difficulties, the offshore groundfishery, source of nearly 40 percent of the weight and nearly 60 percent of the value of New England landings, did so badly that the decline dominated all industry statistics and perceptions of the industry's condition. Indeed, the offshore groundfishery... and the dealers who bought their catch, faced deeper, more prolonged difficulties during the 1950s and 1960s than during the Depression....Falling revenues, declining wages, and shrinking vessel profits quickly ended postwar hopes in most parts of the offshore industry (Dewar 1983:15, 24).

The landings declined sharply in that period, much of the decline due to haddock landings which fell from 60,800 mt in 1965 to 3,700 mt in 1974. To compensate, the vessels turned to codfish which increased in landings from 16,000 mt in 1965 to 25,000 mt in 1976. But then because of rising consumer demand and reduced groundfish supplies, prices were rising and "By the mid-1970s real income in the offshore groundfishery was greater than at anytime since World War II....The average gross return for an otter trawl vessel... increased by more than 30 percent between 1974 and 1976, well ahead of growth and inflation in the rest of the economy" (Doeringer, Moss, and Terkla 1986:20). According to those authors, the combined value of New England finfish and shellfish landings increased sixty-three percent from 1972 to 1976. And then in 1977 groundfish landings rose 21,000 mt above the catch of 1976, an increase of about thirty-four percent. On large offshore vessels average crew share rose twenty-five percent; a crewman could earn $25,000 a year, about twice the earnings of a manufacturing worker. "Average annual earnings in the fishing industry increased by 30 percent in New Bedford between 1976 and 1979 and 35 percent in Gloucester" (Doeringer, Moss, and Terkla 1986:26). This relative prosperity came after nearly forty years of hard times in the fishing industry.

No wonder fishermen were shocked and outraged to learn in the summer of 1977 that the quotas imposed by the council would shut off this long-delayed and newly realized prosperity, particularly with the removal of foreign vessels considered to be the cause of the hard times of the 1960s. The facts that the fleets of hundreds of foreign vessels operating in concert no longer scattered the fish and that the fish were once again schooling and easier to find and catch "proved" to the fishermen that the scientific assessments of depleted stocks were wrong and that there was no justification for strict quotas and trip limits.

The search for solutions begins

It was in this confrontational atmosphere at its September meeting that a number of options were discussed by the council, including proposals from fishermen's groups. In this period, also, there began to be talk within the council about possible limited entry into the fishery; that is, to restrict access to the stocks to only a certain number of designated fishermen, with the purposes of controlling fishing effort or fishing mortality upon the stocks and preventing extended closures. At a public meeting in September, the council's executive director expressed the view that license limitations were inevitable. But such a new regulation, with its many economic and social ramifications, could not of course have been implemented rapidly even if the council had thought it was a good idea. The law required public notice and public hearings with extensive and time-consuming review before implementation. But the idea was even then, in the fall of 1977, after the fact - already too late; there had been an estimated forty percent increase in effort in 1977 for codfishing. Dan Arnold, the president of the Massachusetts Inshore Draggermen's Association, estimated that there had already been a fifty percent increase in vessel tonnage - "new fishermen and the many new and larger boats." Talk of the possibility of limited entry had the predictable result; there was an increase of approximately fifty percent in the number of license applications to harvest groundfish from 1977 to

1978. The increase in groundfish permits from December 1977 to December 1978 was in part "because of the fear of limited entry." [13] The mere talk of limited entry leads fishermen to fear that they will be prevented from fishing and so precipitates a rush for licenses or permits. Holding a license or permit maintains a fisherman's options or flexibility to fish various species as they naturally fluctuate in numbers. (The State of Maine had experienced exactly the same increase when there was talk at about the same time to limit the number of lobster licenses.) Once issued, licenses were not easily revoked.

No management proposal aroused so much anger and so much opposition from the fishing industry and from many members of the Council as any suggestion of limiting entry. The opposition was so strong that the Council could not discuss alternative forms for a program; they argued only about whether they should even consider limiting entry....While the management problems that they had confronted with quotas made the beginning of debate on the variety of limited entry possibilities very reasonable, political opposition made such a dialogue virtually impossible (Dewar 1983:179, 181).

NEFMC and NMFS confrontations

Finally, the council voted to recommend increases in the allowable trip limits of bycatches of cod. Because the council itself cannot promulgate regulations - under MFCMA only the federal government can do that - the recommendations were forwarded to Washington. *Six weeks* later NMFS responded and told the council the increased limits would be allowed, and NMFS added some modifications of its own - but without consultation with the council. NMFS had added increases in haddock and yellowtail catches, removed restrictions on discards (fish thrown

---

[13] Information Memorandum from Terry L. Leitzell, Assistant Administrator, NMFS, to Richard A. Frank, Administrator, NOAA, March 28, 1979.

away because they could not be legally landed), and removed limitations on recreational catches. The result was to weaken the groundfish plan.

> No one on the Council or in the industry could figure out who had made the changes or why, but both Council members and fishermen came away from meetings with NMFS and NOAA [14] directors convinced that NMFS officials in the regional office and in Washington were trying to undermine the Council and take over fishery management (Dewar 1983:163).

This was the first instance of a continuing debate between the council and NMFS as to their relative roles; was the council responsible for writing management plans, or was it simply an advisory body? [15]

> Thus the fishery limped toward the end of 1977 - a year that made painfully clear the difficulties, confrontations, and frustrations that lay ahead. And in fact the fishery was closed by NMFS for the last ten days of year. Officials at NMFS and NOAA imposed the closure without consulting the council, but since the closure came in the holiday season, when most boats were usually in port, it had minimal impact on the fishing industry other than making it clear that the federal government *could* shut it down. The closure outraged council members and fishermen. "Fishermen harvested so few fish in the last week of the year that closure served no conservation purpose. 'This isn't conservation, it's a slap in the face' [said Edward MacLeod, the chairman of the council]. 'It's incredible to

---

[14] NMFS is located within NOAA, National Oceanic and Atmospheric Administration, in the Department of Commerce.

[15] Years later the opinion was expressed by the federal government that the councils could not be sued in court because they are only advisory to NMFS.

close a fishery for a week for nothing'" (Dewar 1983:167).

This was the second instance in 1977 and just one in a series of events of increasing tension between NEFMC and NMFS. In a dispute over the meaning of Optimum Yield, the council chairman in January 1978 stated that "despite guarantees [the chairman cited the guarantees] that Optimum Yield is a guideline only and flexibility is a council prerogative, NMFS is trying to put it in a rigid mold... Optimum Yield remains a vague concept... flexibility is important." [16] Four months later the council complained that NMFS news releases did not conform to council recommendations and wondered where the changes were made. Over two years later Dykstra stated to the council:

> In a recent article in the Nautilus Press an anonymous Washington official was quoted as saying "The New England council is just trying to be good guys to the fishermen. The council has not yet accepted the responsibility for good management." This kind of statement stems from either ignorance or malice... I am not attempting to be a good guy... This council has come far out in front of other councils in attempting to solve some very difficult problems, and we may not look good because we are making that attempt. I resent any official in Washington saying that we are not accepting our responsibility and are being good guys. [17]

David Pierce (MS 1982:23) summarized the first year of the council's experience.

> The first full year... was clearly a learning process and many problems arose along the way. The Council's most contentious and unsolvable problem was the need to conserve and rebuild the cod, haddock, and yellowtail

---

[16] council minutes, January 18-19, 1978

[17] council minutes, July 30, 1980:15

flounder resources without creating economic hardships for the industry. The wisdom of Solomon seemed to be a prerequisite to sieve out fact from fiction amongst the din and cry of fishermen on the one hand and advice of scientists on the other.

This... difference in opinion, seeming impossible deadlines to meet, an uncertainty of the exact administrative procedures necessary to insure timely implementation of Plans and their changes, apparent Council-NMFS/NOAA misunderstandings of each other's intents and motivations, vagueness of the OY concept, and inexperience of many Council members as fishery managers all appeared to contribute towards a general decline in Council morale and a poor decision-making process. It caused a lack of confidence by the industry that the Council could ever extract itself from its problems or that it would ever be able to see the light at the end of the tunnel.

A new plan for 1978

The council recognized clearly that the 1977 plan which it had accepted and adopted without much thought had serious problems and that it had to be replaced with a more effective plan to attain OY for 1978. It began that effort in October 1977, but because of the various procedural requirements of the law and factors over which the council had no control, a new plan could not be prepared in time to be in effect in January 1978. Therefore at the request of the council the federal government by emergency regulation extended the 1977 plan into the first quarter of 1978. If it had not done so, there would have been no plan at all in effect, and there would have been unregulated fisheries.

The events of September through December 1977 contained all the elements of management problems the Council would face in 1978. However, the controversy and difficulty in managing the groundfish increased tremend-ously after the first few months [of 1978]... The race for fish was more intense than during the spring and summer of 1977 because the fishermen understood better that they had to catch fish before others did or lose their opportunity when the fishery closed again. Fishing pressures were also more intense because new fishermen and new boats steadily entered the industry (Dewar 1983:168).

The 1978 plan included all the provisions of the original plan, with the annual species quotas modified on the basis of the latest stock assessments from NMFS. That is, the council's intent was to attain an Optimum Yield (in fact a simple quota) based upon the recommendations of NMFS scientists for acceptable fish catches leading, hopefully, to stock restorations. And the council looked for ways to slow the landings and to distribute the quotas more equitably among the various size classes of fishing vessels. As an example of the council efforts, groundfish committee recommendations are included in Appendix 1. The 1978 plan included trip limits for each species according to the sizes of vessels; thus, for example, vessels of 51-125 gross tons would be limited to 2,500 pounds of cod or haddock landed weight per day or ten percent by weight of the total catch.

But there were more powerful forces in 1978 than in 1977 working against effective constraints upon the catch.

Profits and wages in the groundfish industry were exceptionally high in 1977 and 1978, especially for the offshore industry. The entry of many new boats into the industry was inevitable and probably would have doomed any quota system sooner or later; only the speed with which it happened was surprising (Dewar 1983:177).

Again, the landings of the regulated species rapidly approached the annual quotas in spite of quarterly allocations and allocations by vessel classes and limits on landings per trip. "The Council's management led to overfishing for several reasons. The quota system encouraged fishermen to catch fish as fast as possible in order the get their share before someone else did" (Dewar

1983:158). As the landings approached the quotas, the council and NMFS reduced the trip limits, trying to slow down the catch to make the quotas last throughout the year. But there came a point at which the trip limits were too low to support a fishing vessel; they amounted, in fact, to an economic closure.

A major reason many fishermen caught more than the allowable bycatch [or trip limit] was that the fish really were not bycatch. Fishermen continued to direct their efforts toward groundfish rather than toward other species....Rather than switch to other fisheries as they might have done with a fall in the prices for groundfish, fishermen pressed the Council for more leeway in what was really still a directed fishery (Dewar 1983:160).

During this period economists were studying the New England industry and the possibilities of re-employing displaced fishermen. "If it were true that adjustment [of unemployed fishermen] is easy, efficient management would require a stricter limit on the resources devoted to fishing and on the amount of catch than if the redeployment of resources is difficult. As this book demonstrates, this assumption of flexibility is wrong." And "Our findings suggest that if current management approaches are continued, catch allowances should be more liberal than what would be efficient under the assumption of perfect resource mobility" (Doeringer, Moss, and Terkla 1986:7, 125). Thus was expressed an economic element for the determination of OY as defined by Congress.

Escalating problems and regulations

The period 1978-79 was marked by frequent threats of closures and actual closures of fisheries in various areas, by revisions to quotas, by adjustments to trips limits for three and then four vessel size classes, to specification of trip limits by days at sea, and by the week, and by numbers of men per trip. The regulations rapidly became more complicated and less enforceable because of their increasing complexities. The council searched desperately for tactics that would confine the landings to near the quotas recommended to it by the scientists but that would also avoid closures of fisheries for a month or for two, three, or six months. The council also struggled with the serious problem of substantial and unreported bycatches and discards of regulated species. A senior scientist with NMFS, Vaughan Anthony, reported to the council that discards were the biggest management problem - the problem was "major" and the waste was "terrible." NMFS had estimated from fishermen's reports that the possible discards in the late summer and fall of 1977 was *two or three times* (approximately 63 million young fish) the landings of marketable haddock (Pierce MS 1982:72).

The council tried to deal with this situation by setting up certain areas - "large mesh areas" - in which only mesh of 5 1/8 inches could be used, through which, presumably, juvenile fish could escape. To make this enforceable, NMFS insisted that only one mesh size be permitted on a vessel in that area. But vessels do not fish exclusively in single areas, nor do many of them fish only for regulated species, and species that can only be caught with smaller meshes occur in significant numbers in "large mesh areas." It was estimated, for example, that the redfish fishery, a small-mesh fishery not included in the regulations, would be reduced by twenty-four percent if it were prohibited from fishing in large mesh areas. The council concluded that only one mesh on board would be impractical because of the mixed fisheries nature of New England's groundfish fishery, and wasteful of fuel - this just after the time of the Arab oil boycott - because a vessel would have to return to port, perhaps 200 miles away, to change its mesh size. And there were ways of circumventing "one-mesh-onboard" regulations. One legal mesh inside a second legal mesh in fact produces a sub-legal mesh size. In 1991 the council learned that "net strengtheners" were being used in such a way as to obstruct mesh openings and thus create smaller meshes. And later the council became aware that a few fishermen were perfecting "twisted meshes." When out of the water such a mesh would meet the legal size requirement, but when in the water it would twist in such a way as to present a significantly smaller mesh opening to the fish.

A flood of regulations

It was a period of confusion, contradiction, and haste in rule-making, frustration, disillusion, and chaos. Here, to illustrate the regulatory turmoil, is a summary list of *some* regulatory changes that occurred until the council's Interim Plan, which we will consider shortly, eliminated quotas.

1977
July 8 - Gulf of Maine cod closure
August 22 - Georges Bank cod closure
September 7 - modified trip limits per day for each vessel class
1978
April 13 - cod closure
May 7 - cod, haddock, yellowtail trip limits reduced
June 22 - cod, haddock trip limits reduced
August 5 - some vessels prohibited from cod in Gulf of Maine
September 16 - yellowtail trip limits reduced
November 16 - landings changed to per person per trip
November 17 - haddock closure, cod trip limits reduced
December 17 - haddock trip limits reduced
1979
January 1 - new quotas
February 4 - some cod and haddock fisheries closed, trip limits
    reduced
March 13 - cod and haddock trip limit reductions
April 22 - cod and haddock fisheries closed
April 28 - yellowtail fishery closed
July 22 - cod fisheries closed
October 1 - new quotas
1980
April 13 - yellowtail closure
September 7 - trip limit reductions
October - new quotas

1981
April 10 - trip limit reductions

This is not a record of the council acquiescing to demands of the fishing industry. It is a record of the council trying to achieve the landings limits recommended by NMFS scientists.

In May 1978 the U.S. Coast Guard representative on the council had told the council, not for the last time, that the regulations that had been put in place were "unenforceable." The Coast Guard, with the responsibility for at-sea enforcement, believed the regulations were complicated, confusing, occasionally ambiguous, and far too time-demanding for the Coast Guard's limited capabilities and with its increasing responsibilities in other high-priority areas. "And the limited ability of the NMFS and U.S. Coast Guard," reported Weber (2002:87), "to enforce quotas encouraged wide-spread misreporting and poaching, further undermining confidence in the new management system." But no one proposed simpler, enforceable, effective regulations. In June 1978 council members asserted that there was "no solution" to the seemingly intractable issues.

In July, NMFS told the council that further reductions in trip limits would be necessary to avoid a closure. The council considered such reductions unacceptable, and to avoid another shut-down the council voted to "re-start the clock"; that is, to assume that no fish had been taken to date in 1978 so that the industry would again have the full quotas to work from. The council's rationale for this action was that the existing plan, or rather regulations, had been implemented in a piecemeal and crisis-driven fashion; that the quotas should begin when the full plan was implemented and given a reasonable chance to work. By "re-starting the clock" the OYs were in effect raised.

Margaret Dewar (1983:159) wrote;

> Even if the Council and the Secretary of Commerce had not raised optimum yield, the resources would have been

overfished. NMFS could not enforce the management measures. The small number of NMFS officers could not patrol the unloading of every boat each day....Fishermen learned quickly that they could land more fish than the regulations allowed without being caught....[it was estimated that] only 20 percent of Gloucester skippers were obeying the regulations as of October 1977.

Dykstra had recognized early in 1978 that the prevailing management system would become ever more complicated and of doubtful benefit to the fish, and he tried to develop a simpler and more effective alternative for consideration. He made four points:

1) The existing system demanded more and increasingly reliable stock assessments – to the point that the accuracy demanded becomes uneconomic.

2) The proliferation of regulations to manage all the stocks separately would eventually cause the system to collapse in disarray.

3) Enforcement would become uneconomic and logistically impossible.

4) Increasingly complicated limited entry schemes would destroy the free enterprise character of the fisheries.

Dykstra outlined as an alternative a system of positive and negative economic *incentives* and *disincentive* to direct fishing effort to plentiful stocks and away from stressed stocks. Fishermen would be paid a bonus for landing plentiful species and would be charged an assessment for landing depleted stocks. The assessments would pay for the bonuses. His proposal would have no gear restrictions and no trip or annual limitations, and would induce no discards (*Maine Commercial Fisheries*, September 1978:4). The proposal got little or no attention or further consideration, probably because the council was overwhelmed with trying to respond to the problems of the existing plan. We will return to this idea of a simpler management concept later in this discussion.

Acknowledging failure and a new start

By this time, July 1978, the council's energies and resources were consumed in trying to respond to the latest groundfish crisis - even while it was trying to develop plans for other species. But the council had fully recognized that the original plan was a failure, and that a new start and a new approach were necessary, that the council had to develop an entirely new plan that would try to solve the many problems that had become apparent in its first year and a half. It had in fact directed its staff in May 1978 to begin that task. This new plan would be known as The Northeast Multispecies Fishery Management Plan, but its name was changed a year later to Atlantic Demersal Fisheries (ADF) Plan. The council, for the first time, had raised the question "what are our management objectives - what are we trying to accomplish?" It recognized that the lack of clear objectives in the 1977 plan made it impossible to estimate the consequences of various management options or to measure progress toward even implicit goals. It took several special meetings for the purpose, but the objectives for the plan were agreed to by July 1978. The overall objective, the council decided, "...shall be to generate over the period of the plan the greatest possible joint economic and social net benefits from the harvesting and utilization of the groundfish resource, ensuring that by the end of the period the relevant groundfish stocks shall be in conditions which will produce enhanced and relatively stable yields from the groundfish fishery in future years." Within this broad statement of purpose lay a number of issues that had to be clarified. What were "economic and social net benefits," and who should benefit, and how should the benefits be measured? What conditions would "produce enhanced and relatively stable yields?"

Although phrased in general terms requiring further clarification, this statement of purpose was not a casual, "motherhood" declaration. It was a very thoughtfully and carefully produced policy position, evolved from extended discussion between the council and its staff, taking into account the scientific and political realities they had encountered in the first year. The staff would have to use the statement of purpose as its foundation and guide in producing a complex and difficult multispecies management plan, and the council would have to defend it and live with its consequences. It is to be noted that it made no reference, explicit or implicit, to the concept of "maximum sustainable yield" (MSY) referred to in MFCMA as a biological point of departure for calculating OY. This was deliberate. The council and staff knew by then that MSY was, as we shall see, scientifically unrealistic and irrelevant to New England's multispecies groundfish fisheries.

The council also developed a number of sub-objectives:

1) Prevention of abrupt changes in the relative shares of domestic user-groups in the resources.

2) Freedom of decision-making and choice for individual participants in the fishery should be maintained to the greatest extent possible.

3) Inducement of diversification in the groundfish fishery towards increased utilization of species other than cod, haddock, and yellowtail flounder.

4) minimization of management regulations, subject to attainment of the overall objective.

5) Minimization of enforcement costs, subject to attainment of the overall objective.

6) Provision for accurate and consistent economic, social, and biological data required to monitor effectively and assess the performance of the fishery relative to the overall objective.

Later we shall outline a management proposal that could attain each of these sub-objectives.

The goals represented a significant improvement over the plan of March 1977. The goals were explicit; the Council discussed and agreed upon them, and the Council and the staff could refer back to them in later decisions. The new goals represented the Council's aims better than the original implicit goal to rebuild or stabilize the fish resource without causing undue economic hardship because the overall objective emphasized economic and social benefits rather than fish stocks (Dewar 1983:173).

Even so, unanswered questions remained within the objectives (as distinct from the goals). Margaret Dewar identified the essential but very difficult task of identifying efficacious fisheries management objectives.

The council's vague definition of objectives was understandable. They had had considerable difficulty specifying goals at all. Going farther would prove even harder because the members who represented groups with different interests would clash. More specific definitions would also draw the opposition of interest groups who observed the activity of the Council because the Council could never satisfy everyone.

Even a group working in an apolitical setting would have had trouble making goals more specific, however. Such work required a stronger ideological framework and value judgments, guided by that ideology, about the importance of some styles of fishing compared with others. It required considerable knowledge of the fisheries, especially of the social and economic character of the many groups that harvested groundfish. No one had that knowledge; only massive new data collection and frequent socioeconomic studies could provide the Council with adequate understanding for good planning. Indeed, those who understood most about the industry, some of them on the Council, only became more impressed with the complexity of the issues as the Council confronted crises and tried to formulate a stronger plan. Planning for the use of the fisheries constituted an enormous, immensely complicated intervention in the structure of an industry, in the level and distribution of income in the industry, and in the nature of communities dependent on the industry.

The complexity of the task seemed even more troubling as the staff prodded the Council to move from listing goals to discussing alternative management measures. By April 1979 the Council still had not decided on management measures....Part of the explanation for the delay was that the Council and its Groundfish Oversight Committee spent enormous amounts of time handling the same recurring crises in the new fishing year (Dewar 1983:173-5).

The council recognized, given the requirements of MFCMA for a plan to be acceptable to the federal government, that it would take considerable time - a matter of years, not months - to develop a wholly new plan. At the same time the council had to try to deal with the myriad of problems inherent in the original and still legally binding groundfish plan. It may be noted that these kinds of problems were not unique to the New England council. Weber (2002:61), in a review of various international fisheries conservation organizations to which the United States was a partner, noted:

> As fishing fleets grew, the effectiveness of these and other treaty organizations was challenged by several persistent problems: the difficulty of achieving agreement on meaningful conservation measures among nations with different views, conflicting goals of development and conservation, risk-prone decision-making... resistance to effective enforcement, the failure to support or act on scientific analysis, inadequate funding, and the lack of effective monitoring programs.

And the New England council did not have the support and

diplomatic skills of the State Department to assist it in finding its way through this thicket of common problems.

Adding to the difficulties of developing a new plan was the fact that the council

> had almost no information on which to base decisions that were certain to have profound effects on income distribution and social institutions. No economic data could show how costs, revenues, and profit positions would change in any sectors of the industry with different management decisions. No one knew how fishermen and their communities might suffer from disruption in some institutions and styles of work. When hundreds of angry fishermen converged on meetings to describe the financial and social problems the Council was causing, they provided the best information available. Biological analyses of the condition of the fish resources did exist, but Council members were often skeptical of their accuracy, and they weighed the economic and social information, however exaggerated in the process of political protest, particularly heavily (Dewar 1983:166).

In January 1979 there was a widespread perception in the council and in the industry that quota management as such was a failure - too many intractable problems inevitably came from quotas. But the council was obliged to continue to struggle with those problems as long as it had no alternatives to replace quotas. Through the spring of 1979 there were frequent changes to the regulations with diminishing hope of mitigating the problems. Between January 1978 and March 1979 there were twenty-six official notices in the Federal Register for amendments and emergency amendments, extensions of emergency amendments, adjustments to quarterly quotas, and closures of the fisheries. In fact, more than *100* changes were made in the regulations from 1977 to 1982 (Hennessey and Healey 2000:189).

NMFS proposes higher OYs

Contrary to some critics, it was not just the council, allegedly under pressure from the fishing industry, that "arbitrarily" raised OYs. In March 1979 "unexpectedly and to everyone's astonishment, the NMFS Regional Office proposed a new groundfish plan with significantly higher OYs for all species in all areas except for yellowtail flounder" (Pierce MS 1982:57). The increases proposed by NMFS were:

cod - Gulf of Maine	8,500 to 15,000 mt
cod - Georges Bank	22,000 to 42,120 mt
haddock - all areas	14,900 to 50,000 mt
yellowtail - all areas	8,100 to 10,000 mt

The biomass of all groundfish off New England had increased by roughly seventy-five percent from 1975 to 1979. Much of this was due, no doubt, to the departure of the foreign fleets. Some of it may have been a result of the quotas on landings by the New England fleet, however much they may have been exceeded either by recorded landings or by unrecorded bycatches and discarded fish. The increased biomass prevailed for about three years, after which there was a sharp decline for two years followed by later declines.

There were conditions attached to the NMFS proposal for increased OYs, the most significant of which was that the council should *consider* freezing groundfish permits. In addition, NMFS proposed new trip limits, a limit on the number of men on board vessels, only one mesh of larger size (5 1/2") on board, higher minimum fish size regulations, and state regulations on groundfish in waters under state jurisdiction. This was an all-or-none package proposal from NMFS to the council. Perhaps the higher OYs were bait to get the council to adopt the other measures, including the freeze on new permits.

The council at that time voted to prepare an amendment to

increase OYs, but *less* than those proposed by NMFS because it thought the NMFS proposed increases unwarranted. The council also voted to further consider the other NMFS proposals. Nearly all the NMFS recommendations, agreed to by the council's groundfish committee, were, however, after further discussion, rejected by the council in April,[18] including the moratorium on new fishing permits. (Interestingly, a congressional report in 1990 made the following comment; "In April 1990, the Commerce Committee received a letter signed by more than 200 well-known fishery scientists calling for an immediate moratorium on entry to all major fisheries of the United States." But Congress did not see fit to adopt the recommended moratorium (Bean and Rowland 1997:191)).

In August 1979 NMFS acted to further reduce trip limits. "Everyone realized the consequences of reducing trip limits; viz., increased cod discarding as fishermen pursued other species, greater illegal landings, and misreporting, yet under the existing Groundfish Plan there was no other alternative except a complete closure" (Pierce MS 1982:84).

In September, after the required time periods for public hearings and comment, the council submitted a proposed amendment, Amendment 4, to the Secretary of Commerce, for the purpose of raising the OYs and increasing the mesh size, based on the NMFS recommendations of March. But this was not simply an irresponsible action on the part of the council to placate the fishing industry. It was hoped that higher quotas would alleviate some of the many problems, particularly those created by bycatches and discards. As we noted above, NMFS in March had suggested, based on new stock information, significantly higher OYs for cod and haddock in all areas and a moderate increase for yellowtail flounder (Pierce MS 1982:57). But there is some confusion now on the rationale for the recommended OYs. Interestingly, Pierce (MS 1982:59) noted that NMFS "scientists did not share the Regional Office's view on the appropriateness of the management regime, specifically the size of the OYs." But the

---

[18] The council minutes do not indicate the reasons for rejection.

council's proposed amendment stated:

> The Northeast Fishery Center [of NMFS] and the Council concur that this new information supports the OY increases proposed by this action... as well as potential further action to increase the haddock and yellowtail flounder OYs. The Council recognizes that timely action is necessary to alleviate what substantial evidence indicates will be a significant disparity in the exploitation rates between cod and haddock (which will result in closures and subsequent discarding of haddock this summer) if the haddock OY is not increased. The yellowtail flounder fishery west of 69 W. longitude is already closed for the remainder of the fishing year, despite the expectation of continued high catches and landings which are biologically justifiable based on this recent stock assessment information. The Council has been informed [by NMFS] however, that it is not procedurally possible to take action in this current amendment (#4) to increase the OYs beyond the originally proposed levels.

This proposed all-or-none amendment was not initially considered approvable in part because reviewers in Washington apparently believed that the larger mesh size proposed by the council (without a restriction for "only-one-mesh-size-on-board") was unenforceable. The council wondered why the existing smaller mesh-size regulation (which permitted more than one size on board) was considered to be enforceable but the larger mesh size was not. And Chris Weld, a council member prominently associated with marine conservation movements, said: "There has to be a way of allowing a boat to carry more than one mesh size and still be enforceable." The Regional Administrator replied: "I agree. There are many other ways to make enforceability of mesh size practical and still allow more than one mesh on board." [19] (In the spring of 1981, in fact, the Coast Guard stated to the council that a mesh size of a net *in the water* is enforceable.) The

---

[19] council minutes, January 16-17, 1980

amendment was still in the process of final rule-making in February 1980 and was, after all, implemented in August 1981, almost two and a half years after NMFS made the proposal for the principal component, higher OYs, for this amendment. By this time the OYs recommended in 1979 could well have been out of date; indeed, NMFS approval of the NMFS-proposed increases in OYs came just as the biomasses began a decline that continued until the mid 1990s.

And note the dilemma the council tried to address in this proposed amendment: if cod OY could be raised on the basis of scientific advice, then haddock OY also had to be raised to prevent unrecorded bycatches and discards of more haddock which would inevitably be taken as the otter trawls caught more codfish.

In fact, wrote Margaret Dewar (1983:176), "the Council's progress stalled [because] the members could not figure out what to do. The task was so difficult intellectually and politically that the Council discussions began to sound like reruns of the debates from the two years before."

The notorious Interim Plan

In August and September 1979, because of all those intractable difficulties, a basic change in management measures - a new plan - was recommended as a temporary relief from the continuing troubles. Over two council meetings the new concept was formally moved, debated at length, and adopted, but not unanimously, by the council. As David Pierce (MS 1982:81) noted:

> The plan was considered by many to be a new approach to management and a better alternative to the current plan which 'has led to problems for which there are no solutions, issues which cannot be resolved, and an environment in which even the most rational measures are not accepted.'....
> The tenor of the Plan was that reasonable, acceptable management measures to the industry would foster

compliance and need little enforcement.

Then work began on the so-called Interim Plan (IP). [20] Hopefully it would replace the original groundfish plan, the source of so many intractable problems, and remain in effect only until ADF, the preparation of which would take several years, could be implemented. The Interim Plan was intended to be a short-term, simple, easily enforced plan that would provide some protection to the stocks and that would eliminate the causes of the many problems that had plagued the council and the management process since the early summer of 1977. Its main components were mesh regulations, minimum fish sizes, and two long-standing closed areas. As proposed, it had no quotas or trip limits. The proponents acknowledged that it carried the risk that those simple measures might not be sufficient to prevent stock declines, and it was neither intended nor expected that the plan would lead to stock rebuilding or management in a conventional sense.

The purpose of the Interim Plan has been much misunderstood. Hennessey and Healey (2000:199), for example, stated that the IP depended upon minimal measures "to ensure stock conservation and rebuilding." Such is not the case, as we have noted. Michael Weber (2002:93) stated that the plan "used Orwellian logic in defining OY for the fishery as being whatever amount was actually caught." Indeed, the plan did define OY in just that way, but *not* for the purpose of permitting an open, unrestricted fishery. The purpose of the council was not, as Weber stated, to impose "as little regulation as possible," but rather to give the council

---

[20] Fordham (1996) states that the Interim Plan was adopted by the council in response to industry pressure to eliminate the quota system. Similarly, Weber (2002:93) states that the council adopted the plan under pressure from the fishing fleet. These statements are not correct. In fact, the plan came entirely from within the council, not from industry pressure. And segments of fishermen "feared" the plan. "Spokesmen for fishermen and fishing vessel owners... repeated unwavering opposition to the plan. One said... he feared 'disaster'." New Bedford (MA) Standard Times. Feb. 6, 1982.

itself the opportunity to design a truly effective stock restoration and management plan. Optimum Yield had to be defined as it was in IP if the plan were to accomplish its primary purpose; any numerical definition of OY would have led inexorably once again to the numerous problems of quotas that the council had experienced since 1977 and which had led to the failure of the plan of 1977. The primary purpose of IP was simply to get the council away from day-to-day responses to seemingly never-ending crises and, most importantly, to give the council time to re-think its purposes and strategies that would be incorporated into ADF which, hopefully, would indeed be a plan that would rebuild and maintain the stocks.

Initially the proponents of the Interim Plan hoped that because of its intended simplicity it could be prepared and implemented in a few months. But it was then recognized that because of the legal requirements of MFCMA, IP could not be implemented for at least a year. In fact, for those and other reasons which we will consider, it took nearly three years.

Regulations without end

In the meantime, the council tried repeatedly by a bewildering combination of regulations to slow the landings of fish. The regulations had indeed become complex. Weber (2002:xvii) noted, with reference just to the plan for the relatively simple monkfish fishery, that

> the complexity of the fishery led to great complexity in management measures. Not only did some fishermen use different kinds of fishing gear to catch monkfish for market, but also, other fishermen incidentally caught monk-fish that they might sell or discard. Each group of fishermen would have to be managed somewhat differently. Equitably allocating catch among these different types was

fraught with controversy. [21]

Council member James O'Malley characterized the monkfish plan as "excruciatingly" complicated (CFN July 2000:8A).

Weber's comment on complexity applied with even greater relevance to the evolution of regulations for the much more complex New England groundfish fishery that used a variety of gear types and included at least a dozen species and distinct stocks which were to a considerable degree intermixed in unequal proportions on the fishing grounds, and the status of which impinged significantly upon a number of other fisheries, such as scallops, shrimp, herring, quahogs, and lobsters. This reality was acknowledged by NMFS: "This complexity is a *major* contributor to the difficulties of fishery management in New England" (emphasis added). [22] It is a serious mistake to think of New England groundfish as a simple, easily characterized, and easily managed fishery. It is not.

At the beginning of 1980, existing regulations, in the words of David Pierce (MS 1982:71), "were very confusing and difficult to apply in practice." And he gave examples arising from the mixed-species nature of the otter trawl fishery. This reality was one of the reasons for attempting to develop the Interim Plan as rapidly

---

[21] In 2001, NOAA/NMFS stated "The condition of the monkfish stocks off the New England and Mid-Atlantic coast has improved significantly over the last 3-4 years under the Council's joint management program with the Mid-Atlantic Council. Fishing removals are declining and target harvest rates and associated management measures are projected to end overfishing and continue stock rebuilding... northern stocks of monkfish [are] no longer overfished" Anon. 2001. Conserving America's Marine Fisheries: a Quarter Century of Progress. Regional Fishery Management Councils and NOAA Fisheries.

[22] Information Memorandum from Terry L. Leitzell, Assistant Administrator, NMFS, to Richard A. Frank, Administrator, NOAA, March 28, 1979.

as possible.

In the spring of 1980 the council tried again to respond to the groundfish problems within the existing plan. It proposed Amendment 5 to revise haddock and yellowtail OYs based on most recent NMFS stock assessment information. "The new haddock OY would be 44,125 MT, a 35.8% increase over OYs specified in Amendment #4. A new yellowtail OY was to be approximately 20,000 MT and represented a 100% increase in the OY specified in Amendment #4" (Pierce MS 1982:78). The council also proposed in this amendment an administrative mechanism to allow the setting of OYs to reflect current stock conditions and not be "306 to 450 days out of phase with relevant assessment information" (Pierce MS 1982:78). OY values would be adjusted, not under industry pressure, but automatically according to scientific criteria in response to assessed changes in stock biomass. The council approved Amendment 5 at its September 1980 meeting. It was implemented one year later, a rather ironic time-delay considering that the measure was intended to make possible *timely* responses to changing stock conditions. Years before, Lee Alverson, then Director of the Northwest Fisheries Center of NMFS, had noted that "Management is a matter of making decisions and it is often important to make a decision in time as to make precisely the best decision" (Alverson 1972:214).

Six months after it adopted the new concept of IP, the council expressed its frustration and anger at the time taken to develop and implement this or any plan. "The necessity of Washington NMFS to mull over all council recommendations to 'insure legality' and 'to keep within the intent of the Fishery Management Act' before accepting and implementing them, prohibited real-time management actions and did not serve to reduce the communication, as well as credibility, gaps between the council and Washington" (Pierce MS 1982:31).

NMFS: "There may not be a solution"

Fifteen months after the council expressed its intent to adopt the new plan there were new attempts to speed up the review and implementation process. Early in 1981 the council and NMFS were sued by a large fishing company on the grounds that the proposed plan was based on bad information, and was ineffective and discriminatory. In March 1981 it was reported to the council that large boats were taking much more than their quota under the original 1977 plan, and that unrecorded landings of yellowtail flounder were much in excess of the limits. The Regional Administrator for NMFS told the council "We have come to recognize that there may not be a solution to the groundfish management situation." [23]

The Interim Plan received initial council, but not federal, approval in June 1981, almost two years after it had been proposed (final council approval came in September 1981), and the council again complained against inexplicable delays in implementing amendments to the existing plan. At just this time (July 29, 1981) Malcolm Baldridge, the Secretary of Commerce himself, wrote to the council [24] urging that it expedite preparation of IP and submit it for review by October 1, 1981. The secretary wrote that vessels were

> disadvantaged by the present management system... should [not] have to operate under the present management system any longer than is necessary to implement an acceptable substitute. Accordingly....I will instruct my staff to expedite its review to the maximum extent permitted by law.

---

[23] council minutes, March 24, 1981

[24] Letter from Malcolm Baldridge, Secretary of Commerce, to Robert A. Jones, Chairman of the New England Fishery Management Council, July 29, 1981.

The council submitted the plan for review on November 2, 1981. NMFS then advised the council that, in spite of the secretary's letter to the council and his instructions to his staff, the federal government review of IP would take at least nine months and perhaps a year even though the Regional Administrator of NMFS and his staff had of course participated in all the council and committee discussions for the development of IP. But early in 1982 the council was notified that IP would replace the original 1977 plan on April 1. In the meantime some of the industry called the plan a "mixed blessing" because it anticipated, as a result of the "quota-less" plan, a glut of fish and a serious price depression particularly affecting smaller boats.

Interim Plan implemented

The Interim Plan was implemented in April 1982, two years and ten months after its inception, and it remained in effect until 1986 when the ADF plan was partially approved. It had been hoped when first proposed that the IP could be implemented in six months. That, as it turned out, was a naive expectation. The delay was caused in part by the fact that the council itself lost sight of its primary purpose; that the plan was intended to be as *simple* as possible in order to cause a minimum of problems and so that it could be implemented rapidly - all to give the part-time council the capability, without the distractions of monthly crises, to focus on development of the long-term ADF plan. The delay was also the result of:

1) The complexities of the groundfishery, even for a plan of very limited objectives;

2) a concern within the council and the federal government that the plan contained no "fail-safe" or "braking" mechanism - no provision to take effect if stocks declined seriously under the plan (this issue would cause great controversy and considerable delay);

3) the time taken for review by the federal government; and

4) by the administrative and public hearing requirements of the law for plan implementation.

The fishing fleet grows

In the meantime, in 1980, the council had begun work on ADF, the plan that was to replace, as soon as possible, both the NMFS plan of 1977 and the Interim Plan. It should be noted that the problem of effort, or fishing power, in the fishery was now substantially higher in 1980 than it had been in 1977 for reasons over which the council had no control. Weber (2002:87) noted that "The value of quotas... was undermined as new fishing vessels continued entering the fishery at the rate of one every four days." Between 1976 and 1979, the number of medium-sized groundfish vessels grew by seventy-five percent, and the number of trawlers over 125 tons increased by 144 percent (Doeringer, Moss, and Terkla 1986:29; Woodward 2004:223)). The total number of vessels actively fishing off New England had grown from 825 to 1423. From December 1977 to December 1978 commercial groundfishing vessel permits increased from 1,094 to 1,871, "although the number active in the fishery is smaller." [25] The removal of foreign fishing vessels created euphoria within the New England industry, and remarkably increased landings and new profitability encouraged new construction and renovation of fishing vessels.

Two federal programs in particular had encouraged the growth. The Capital Construction Fund, established in 1970, allowed fishermen or vessel owners to defer paying income taxes on profits from their boats if the money were placed in a special account for later renovation or new construction of a vessel. The Fisheries Obligation Guarantee Program, established in 1972, provided government guarantees for loans at lower interest rates (about one half the prevailing rates in the early 1980s) and for

---

[25] Information Memorandum from Terry L. Leitzell, Assistant Administrator, NMFS, to Richard A. Frank, Administrator, NOAA, March 28, 1979

longer pay-back periods to build or upgrade boats. And by 1979 a ten percent tax credit for the 1980s made it too expensive not to buy a boat. An investor who paid $1 million for a boat, regardless of the source of the money, could deduct ten percent or $100,000, from his tax obligations. This incentive was abetted by accelerated depreciation credits.

All kinds of investors, many of whom were not fishermen, bought vessels. Banks encouraged the flood of new money, and they paid for large vessels. The tax credit was ended in 1986, but by then the number of large vessels (over eighty feet in length) had tripled and vessels over 150 tons had increased fivefold. Not only had the number of small and large vessels increased, but the average fishing power of all vessels had also increased. Indeed, all this was consistent with one of the original purposes of MFCMA. Weber (2002:85) stated that "While much of the language of the act had to do with the management of fisheries, the immediate aim of many supporters in Congress, the NMFS, and the industry was to expand U.S. fishing....the Magnuson-Stevens Act loosed an unprecedented expansion of fleets, landings, and exports." In view of the continuing concern by managers and federal fisheries officials in the 1980s and 1990s about overcapitalization in the New England fishing fleet, one may be perplexed by the fact that only in 2004 did the U.S. Commission on Ocean Policy, created by the president of the United States, call for Congress to repeal those financial assistance programs (CFN May 2004:9A).

Atlantic Demersal Fisheries Plan

It was in this environment that the council committees and staff struggled to develop the new plan, ADF. The draft plan was presented to the full council in April 1984 and for the next year it was subject to public hearings and vigorous debate within the council. NMFS disapproved the plan by March 1986. But after some modifications, NMFS, by July 1986, gave partial approval, for one year only; the plan would become effective in September 1986. The partial approval was on the condition that the council within a year adopted further restrictions on the taking of small fish.

The council tried to devise tactics whereby fishermen could continue to fish for those unregulated species such as whiting (silver hake) that required a small mesh without taking large numbers of juvenile fish and regulated species. It made great effort to this end because to deny those opportunities would result in more fishermen directing their efforts to the regulated species; the council was trying to divert effort away from the regulated species. The problem is that the unregulated and regulated species are intermixed in many of the same grounds. The result of the council's efforts was an Optional Settlement Program (OSP) within ADF whereby fishermen, under a number of specific rules, could fish with small meshes within large mesh areas. OSP was soon renamed and known as the Exempted Fisheries Program.

The council after 1986

The history of the council after our terms had expired at the end of 1986 may be summarized by a review of the amendments to the groundfish plan. Its name in later years was changed back from the Atlantic Demersal Finfish Plan to Northeast Multi-species Fishery Management Plan when a new series of numbered amendments began.

In 1987 Amendment 1 to ADF reduced the area for the silver hake exempted fishery and increased the large mesh area to include yellowtail in the south.

As part of ADF, the council had established a Technical Monitoring Group (TMG) - a broad-based group of fisheries scientists - to advise it on the efficacy of ADF. By midsummer of 1988 TMG reported to the council that ADF was "falling far short" (CFN August 1988:10) of the objective to rebuild and maintain stocks. TMG stated that the management *system* was not very effective overall. By system it meant not just the council's management measures which it found in serious need for improvement, but also NMFS's effort and ability to enforce the regulations. A large number of fishermen participating in the Exempted Fisheries Program failed to file required reports; small meshes permitted in the program had led to high levels of discard mortality of juvenile fish; and some fishermen were using the Exempted Fisheries Program to target regulated groundfish with small mesh and were falsifying their reports to cover those actions. According to TMG, spawning closures for yellowtail flounder were not working, and a high percentage of fishermen were not abiding by the 5 1/2-inch mesh requirement in the Gulf of Maine and on Georges Bank. The report said "even when the Coast Guard is on the scene, fishermen have perfected methods of switching nets and/or jettisoning illegal nets before being observed." TMG reported that "only the careless fishermen are caught."

Amendment 2 in February 1989 implemented trip bycatch limits and tougher non-reporting penalties, increased the minimum size for yellowtail flounder and for American plaice, and established a seasonal large mesh area on Nantucket Shoals to protect cod.

Amendment 3 in 1990 established a Flexible Area Action System (FAAS), intended to be a cooperative arrangement with fishermen, in part at their request. When fishermen reported large concentrations of juvenile or spawning fish, temporary closures could be implemented *very quickly* to protect the fish. The FAAS program was tried several times but was not very effective, largely because the administrative review process, perceived by the federal government to be necessary in each case, took so long that the closures were ineffective - too little and too late.

Amendment 4 in 1991 implemented a variety of modifications affecting the small-mesh fisheries, all to protect cod, haddock, and yellowtail. And it defined "overfishing" to conform to so-called "602 guidelines" as provided for in MFCMA and published in 1989 by NMFS. Although titled "guidelines" by Congress, NMFS interpreted them to be binding upon the councils. Every plan and every amendment to a plan must then contain a definition of overfishing, contain management measures to prevent overfishing, and include measures leading to stock rebuilding for overfished stocks. NMFS asserted that any amendment submitted for approval *must* adhere to the guidelines, but in subsequent amendments to MFCMA, Congress clarified its intent for the guidelines by stating "that the guidelines do not have the force and effect of law" (Bean and Rowland 1997:156).

Reinstatement of direct effort controls

Groundfish were reported to be in terrible shape in late 1989, and so NEFMC began the preparation of a new and tougher amendment, including measures for direct controls on fishing effort rather than the indirect controls in the original ADF. This was the beginning of Amendment 5, a significant milestone in the development of New England groundfish management. Because direct controls were necessarily difficult to devise and highly controversial in this complex fishery, their development was time-consuming, but by early 1991 the council had decided upon and publicized the outline of Amendment 5. At about the same time a special groundfish task force created in Massachusetts issued its highly critical report on groundfish management. It advocated, among other measures, the reinstatement of quotas - even with full knowledge of the problems associated with them. A spokesperson for the task force made the following revealing admission: "We supported quotas because we didn't come up with another alternative that would directly affect fishing mortality" (CFN February 1991 17A).

And then in June 1991 the Conservation Law Foundation and the Massachusetts Audubon Society sued the Secretary of Commerce and NMFS for failing to prevent overfishing and failing to rebuild the depleted stocks. The plaintiffs sued those agencies and not NEFMC because the plaintiffs could not find precedent for suing fisheries management councils. By a consent decree the court directed the council to prepare a plan to stop overfishing for public comment by March 1, 1992, and to submit the plan for final approval by September 1, 1992. The decree stated that "overfishing" must be defined and that overfishing on cod and yellowtail flounder must be ended in five years, and on haddock in ten years. The council then had about six months to find a solution to the problem of constraining fishing to OYs with which it had struggled for years. David Pierce (CFN November 1991:11A) noted that the council would be challenged to construct a plan "that will be multispecies while avoiding increased discards, illegal fishing, false reporting, and the chaos that reigned during the late 1970s with poorly designed quota-based management." Neither the plaintiffs themselves nor NMFS offered suggested remedies they considered acceptable solutions to the problem. The director of the Conservation Law Foundation could not claim to know the answer to the problem. He was reported to have said: "We are the first to admit that this is very complicated stuff. We're going to put some serious scientists on this. We're going to really pull out some of the best people we can find in the world to think about these problems" (CFN February 1992:11B). He did not explain how he would accomplish that goal within the six-month time constraint imposed by the consent decree mandating a management plan that would contain the solution. Nor have his other intentions to recruit the "best people" been implemented. It has been stated (Hennessey and Healey 2000:206) that the consent decree ordered the council to prepare Amendment 5. In fact, as we noted, the council on its own initiative had developed the essence of the amendment eighteen months before the legal suit was filed.

The council missed the court-ordered deadlines, but neither party to the consent decree, neither the plaintiffs nor the federal agencies, insisted on the deadlines, perhaps because they did not have an answer to the problem - better to leave it to the council to struggle with the problem.

Not until March 1994 was Amendment 5 implemented. In the amendment the council took some major actions, including a moratorium on new vessel permits during the "rebuilding period," and implementation of a "days-at-sea" (DAS) effort reduction program. This program prohibited vessels greater then forty-five feet in length with a groundfish permit to be at sea for more than a certain number of days per year, the number of permitted days determined by previous vessel fishing history and varying among different size-classes of vessels. The permitted DAS would be reduced by ten percent per year for five years to one half of the days initially allowed. The intent was to achieve a fifty percent reduction in fishing effort by 1999. The limitation on fishing effort by means of DAS was intended to avoid the numerous problems experienced from quota limitations on effort. The amendment included mandatory reporting for landings in addition to other measures. Mesh size was increased to six inches, which fishermen in southern New England, but not in northern New England, had strenuously opposed for years. Two large areas on Georges Bank were closed to fishing. This amendment, primarily because of the DAS provision, was a pivotal action for future management.

Biological reference points

In this period the concept of "biological reference points" (BRPs) emerged as a prominent part of fisheries management plans. BRPs are specific numerical parameters of an existing or desired condition of a stock. Target fishing mortality rates "as well as criteria for stock size, fishing effort, and other features thought to optimize a fishery are often called biological reference points" (Rothschild, Sharov and Lambert 1997:142). For example, maximum spawning potential (MSP), or maximum sustainable yield, or long-term potential yield are BRPs. BRPs were now the *de facto* objectives of management plans and the success of management would be judged upon attaining those reference points. The objective of management, therefore, was (and is) no longer OY, however modified by socioeconomic considerations as mandated by Congress, but was now determined solely by fisheries scientists who calculate the BRPs, with the council relegated to the more controversial and much more difficult position of trying to devise strategies or tactics to attain them.

Stocks hit rock bottom

In the winter and spring of 1994 NMFS told the council that the numbers of haddock in the Gulf of Maine and on Georges Bank were the "lowest on record" (CFN September 1994:1A). The NMFS regional science director stated that "Gulf of Maine haddock is commercially extinct" and that scientists expressed grave concern for the very survival of the species. Yellowtail flounder was reported to be severely depleted. Amendment 6, in June 1994, brought in several measures to further protect haddock. But in the summer of 1994 the Stock Assessment Review Committee (SARC) of NMFS told the council that Amendment 5, five months after review, approval, and implementation by NMFS, could not accomplish its stated purposes of eliminating overfishing and of stock rebuilding (CFN September 1994:18A). The council was told that the spawning stock biomasses of cod, haddock, and yellowtail on Georges Bank had "collapsed," and the NMFS regional science director advised the council that this was a "fifteen- to twenty-year problem" (CFN September 1994:1A). The council therefore began immediate development for a new amendment to implement the recommendations of SARC.

The result was Amendment 7, implemented in July 1996. The amendment accelerated the DAS effort-reduction program from five years to two years, eliminated some exemptions from the effort reduction program, and provided for further protection for juvenile and spawning fish by creating new large-scale closed areas off the coasts of Maine, New Hampshire, and Massachusetts. It changed trip limits for cod and haddock, and reduced target Total Allowable Catch (TAC) for Gulf of Maine cod from 6.1 million pounds to 5.7 million pounds. Trip limits would be reduced to 400 pounds when half the 1998 limit of 3.9 million pounds was taken. The principal purpose of Amendment 7 was to reduce fishing effort on cod, haddock, and yellowtail flounder by *eighty* percent from 1993 levels and cut fishing mortality to as close to zero as practical. Because of these drastic reductions in fishing effort, the council came under substantial political pressures to relent from industry, state legislators, and congressional representatives, including some of New England's senators, but the council resisted the pressure and held to its purpose.

Unintended consequences

Part of the reason for establishing large inshore closed areas was a result - a consequence - of the implementation of the DAS regulations in Amendment 5. Vessels that previously had fished well offshore, on Georges Bank and elsewhere, sought to maximize their DAS fishing time by reducing their steaming time to offshore waters and concentrating their time and efforts in inshore waters. This unintended consequence of course put significant additional pressure on the inshore stocks some of which were on spawning grounds. It also created new competition for the smaller vessels that traditionally fished inshore waters and could not fish offshore, and it led to increased gear conflicts among fishermen.

The council's attention now was increasingly taken up with the problem of escalating gear conflicts, diverting it from the primary job of preventing overfishing and rebuilding stocks. The Coast Guard representative to the council remarked that some of the conflicts were "downright nasty." The conflicts arose as fishermen sought new grounds to fish and thereby encountered fishermen already working those grounds. Fishermen were displaced from their traditional familiar waters by the large area closures on Georges Bank and on Nantucket Shoals, by the scarcity of fish on their traditional grounds, and by running out of their allotted DAS. This last factor caused them to shift onto species (and waters) not included in the DAS program. Amendment 8 was designed to minimize gear conflicts that had increased as a result of the additional regulations.

The council was advised in mid 1997 that with the exception of cod in the Gulf of Maine ("the stock is on the verge of collapse") cod, haddock, and yellowtail stocks on Georges Bank and southern New England were still low but increasing. Following the decline in biomasses in 1985, there had been small recoveries through 1991 followed by severe declines to very low levels through 1994. Thus the reported increases of 1997 were encouraging.

In response to the reported status of cod in the Gulf of Maine in 1997, the council implemented large and highly controversial "rolling closures" by which critical areas in the western Gulf of Maine for spawning cod were closed to fishing at certain seasons. There were also new trip limits for cod and haddock.

All this effort by the council to rebuild Gulf of Maine cod stocks caused great tension and distress in the fishing communities. The anger, frustration, and stress erupted in the ugly, threatening, and "reprehensible" (CFN January 1998:8A) scene at the council meeting of December 1997. And it was to continue.

At this point *Commercial Fisheries News* (June 1999:6A) editorialized that

> The rules have become so complicated and they are changing so often that no one, absolutely no one, can keep track of them all....Even the people at the National Marine Fisheries Service who have to implement the rules admit they can hardly keep up and are having trouble adequately informing fishermen of the latest in the endless stream of changes.

Coast Guard Rear Admiral Richard Larrabee twice appealed for simpler regulations. He stated that the Coast Guard had neither the budget nor manpower to enforce them as written. "Even with the increased manpower, which we have just been granted, we would be unable to check for compliance, given the complexity of the rulings" (Playfair 2002:37).

For the next several years the council would spend much time and great effort trying to address the problem of cod in the Gulf of

Maine. The sizes and locations of several closed areas along the coast would be changed and adjusted in the hope of reducing fishing mortality of the cod, and there were continuing efforts to adjust the trip limits. The problem was one of balancing the intent of keeping fishing effort low to protect the small numbers of cod in the gulf with the hope of reducing the unreported discards and waste of cod taken as incidental catch. If the limits were too low, illegal and unrecorded discards would be high; if the limits were raised, too many cod would be taken to permit stock rebuilding.

More amendments

Amendment 9, in November 1999, added Atlantic halibut to the ADF, included new definitions of overfishing, and set OYs for twelve groundfish species as required by congressional amendments to the MFCMA in 1996. But then in April 2002 the court, maintaining its presence in the process since the consent decree from the law suit of 1991, found that Amendment 9 no longer represented the best available science. The advice that had been the basis of Amendment 9 had been replaced with a new scientific report in March 2002, and so the council had to begin once again the task of restructuring Amendment 13 which it had begun even before Amendment 9 had been implemented.

(Amendment 10 had to do with administrative adjustments to the plan. And Amendment 11, March 1999, designated Essential Fish Habitat for all species as required by amendments to MFCMA in 1996. Amendment 12, March 2000, brought the plan into compliance with amendments of 1996 to MFCMA with respect to whiting, red hake, and offshore hake.)

Amendment 13 and new litigation

The council had begun work on Amendment 13 early in 1999. To meet the stricter overfishing requirements of the 1996 amendments to MFCMA, it had to reduce fishing mortality of Georges Bank cod by thirty percent and by sixty-five percent for yellowtail flounder off southern New England. It also had to respond to the court ruling that Amendment 9 was no longer valid.

A coalition of conservation and environmental groups, which had had a substantial role in the 1996 amendments to MFCMA, issued a report in 2001 that new and drastic changes to MFCMA were needed. It charged that the management councils (plural) had made little attempt to follow the letter or spirit of the law, and that NMFS had approved many management plans that did not comply with the legal mandates and allowed needless and harmful delays (CFN December 2001:9B). Legislation was introduced in Congress to further amend MFCMA.

SARC reported to NEFMC in July 2001 that the biomass of cod in the Gulf of Maine had more than doubled in the two years 1999-2001. The SARC report also stated that fishing mortality was "very high" - approximately three times the recommended level. The SARC report did not explain how the stock could more than double in biomass under very high fishing mortality, and if the council was puzzled by this apparent paradox the news story did not report it (CFN August 2001:9A). In September, two months later, NMFS told the council that in spite of the apparently large increase of cod biomass in the Gulf of Maine in the face of very high fishing mortality, a *sixty-three* percent decrease in fishing mortality was necessary. At this point the dominant role of biological reference points (BRPs) in the management process becomes apparent. The NMFS Regional Administrator told the council: "Our first objective was to meet the Amendment 7 biological targets. We're still targeting Fmax, which is.27, and we're around .7."

According to the SARC, the current fishing mortality rate on Gulf of Maine cod is .73. The objective under Amendment 7 is to achieve a fishing mortality rate of Fmax, which is "the rate of fishing mortality that produces the maximum level of yield per recruit." The Fmax target is .27. The difference between .27 and .73 is staggering. Achieving the lower Fmax rate will require a 63%

reduction in fishing mortality (CFN November 2001:22A).

A new assessment report in the summer of 2005 indicated that cod in the Gulf of Maine and on Georges Bank had declined by over twenty percent. An industry consultant suggested that the decline in the face of more stringent regulations must be due to natural or climactic factors beyond the reach of regulations. An environmental-group representative said the declines must be because the regulations are not strict enough (*Portland Press Herald* August 17, 2005:B3).

In addition to the eight amendments to the groundfish plan since 1994, by 2004 there were also more than forty "framework adjustments" which did not require the full administrative review procedures required for amendments. The adjustments addressed such things as:

- a possession limit for winter flounder minimum mesh size for the whiting fishery on Cultivator Shoals, a part of Georges Bank
- reduction of incidental catch of harbor porpoise
- protection of right whales in the vicinity of Cape Cod
- extensions and additions of closed areas
- adjustments of trip limits for cod and haddock
- adjustments of DAS depending upon the size of mesh used

Amendment 13 was implemented early in 2004 with its "extremely complex" (CFN December 2003:1A) regulations; for example, there were now four categories of permitted "days-at-sea." There then followed five law suits by conservation, environmental, and fisheries groups, each with different complaints about the management plan. A council member was quoted in late 2006 that: "The current management system needs to be simplified. The combination of time, gear and area restrictions is daunting at best and incomprehensible at worst" (CFN Oct. 2006:14B).

In 2006 and 2007 NEFMC, recognizing the problems inherent in the "days-at-sea" concept, invited and gave some consideration to alternative management suggestions – a "points" system, "area management", and an expanded "sector" program. But in 2007, under pressure of mandatory time constraints for plan amendments, the council deferred further consideration of those complicated alternatives and committed itself to further revisions of the "days-at-sea" regulatory policy, even though it was widely regarded as complicated, confusing, and ineffective.[26] Late in 2007 the council reversed itself again and voted to resume work on the "sector" concept. It did this over the strenuous objections of NMFS, which argued that, within the time constraints, there were simply not enough resources to undertake the necessary analysis of both "days-at-sea" and the numerous "sector" proposals before the council.

A pattern of a kind seemed to have emerged by 2004. Law suits, escalating from one to two to five, underlie ever-increasing complexities in the New England groundfish plan, which in turn seem to provide opportunities for further litigation. Amendments to MFCMA which added to the requirements and paperwork burden upon the councils for plan development have increased the opportunities for litigation with the resulting further complexities. Even with the initial legislation there was opportunity for law suits. MFCMA initially had required each council to prepare FMPs for *each* fishery within the area of its jurisdiction. NEFMC of course has not done that, and we would guess that none of the eight councils have met that legal requirement. And it is a curious fact that as NEFMC can show that there have been encouraging increases generally since 1995 in some stocks of groundfish (CFN

---

[26] In December 2006 the fisheries service published "Answers to Commonly Asked Framework Adjustment 42 Questions" (CFN Special Supplement). For example, "If a Day gillnet vessel fishes in the SNE DA for 2.5 hr and outside of the SNE DA for 3 hr, the vessel would be charged for 15 hr because the DAS charge within the SNE DA would be less than the DAS charge if the vessel fished outside the SNE DA for an equivalent time. When fishing in the SNE DA, the vessel would be charged 8 hr (2.5 hr inside SNE DA at 2:1 plus 3 hr outside SNE DA at 1:1), while if the vessel fished outside of the SNE DA, a 5.5 hr trip would have resulted in a 15 hour DAS charge (5.5 hr is between 3-15 hr)."

February 2002:20A), so also there has been a parallel increase in the number of legal actions against its management plans. One must expect from this legal action further adjustments and more complex amendments to be followed by further legal action...

5) A Review of the Problems

A part-time council

Let us try to summarize the position of the council in its first ten years - and in later years, in fact. Council members were all part-time participants, each having full-time responsibilities elsewhere. Nevertheless, with extra committee meetings and with the preparation necessary beforehand - the digestion of numerous and voluminous reports and analyses prepared for them by NMFS and council staff [27] - for effective participation in committee and council meetings, council members experienced ever-increasing demands on their time. The groundfish plan - the only one we consider here - was just one of a number of controversial plans the council had to develop or amend at the same time. The council in its first ten years had a scientific staff of four to assist it in the identification, development, and analyses of plan options (NMFS had a regional staff of more than one hundred). The council did not have exclusive jurisdiction over the stocks for which it was responsible. And there were continuing tensions between NEFMC and NMFS as to whether the council was simply advisory or in fact had management responsibility with congressional authority to exercise its best judgment for management decisions. Neither NEFMC nor NMFS had practical experience, at least in the early years, in the management of multispecies fisheries as required by MFCMA, as shown by the failure of the NMFS-prepared 1977 groundfish plan. The council had no assistance in trying to devise effective and practical management or effort control measures even, as we shall see, from a group of experts specifically

---

[27] We may wonder how many council members absorbed the 1600 pages of Amendment 13.

assembled by NMFS to advise and guide the council toward an effective management plan for groundfish. Indeed, it seems clear in hindsight that in those early years there was a generally held false assumption that persons knowledgeable about fish, or about fisheries science, or fisheries administration, or fishing, or about the fishing industry were therefore knowledgeable about fisheries *management*. It was a distinction that only painful experience would clarify. And the council was confronted with an industry that had deep-seated distrust of the scientific advice on the status of the stocks and which all too often actively resisted the management regulations of the council's plans and found ways for noncompliance. With these circumstances in mind, none of the council's making, the judgment of Dobbs (2002:60) about the "excruciatingly dysfunctional council process" seems unduly harsh and prejudicial to council members but perhaps not to the context in which the council had to function. Years later, Guy Marchessault, the first chief scientist and later Deputy Executive Director of the council, reflected that "Given the initial conditions of ICNAF quotas/trip limits, apparently diminishing stocks, subsidized investment in the fishery, the unwieldy and unresponsive plan generation process, and the frenetic public review process...the council never really established a solid footing to develop its own version of a more enlightened approach to management."

The paperwork burden

We note the observation (Rothschild et al. 1980:1), made three years after the beginning of MFCMA, as an indication of the bureaucratic requirements within which the council had to act and as an indication of why it was so difficult for the council to act in a timely manner on the numerous problems that confronted it: "It was evident that the evolving regulatory regime would be rife with time-consuming, redundant, and costly paperwork." This paperwork burden arose from the requirement of MFCMA as enacted that each council "shall prepare... a management plan with respect to *each* fishery within its geographical area of authority" (emphasis added). Thus the council was legally required to produce a plan for a fishery, whether it had conservation or management problems or not. And the burden arose in part from the fact that by law each plan had to abide by an intimidating array of specified legal requirements. The introduction to Amendment 13 in 2003 states:

> In preparing a Fishery Management Plan, the Council must comply with the requirements of the National Environmental Policy Act (NEPA), and Regulatory Flexibility Act (RFA), the Administrative Procedures Act (APA), the Paperwork Reduction Act (PRA), the Coastal Zone Management Act (CZMA), the Data Quality Act (P.L. 106-554), and Executive Orders 12612 (Federalism), 12630 (Property Rights), 12866 (Regulatory Planning), 12898 (Environmental Justice), and 13158 (Marine Protected Areas).

A maze of terminology

Let us consider the point of departure for the operation of the fishery councils; that is to say, the policy guidance, instructions, and procedures from Congress to the councils for fishery management. A report to the New England council in early 1977 by the consulting firm Developmental Sciences (Anon. MS 1977) characterized the environment in which the councils were to function:

- The council must function within a paperwork nightmare. FMPs [Fishery Management Plans] require *at the very least* exhaustive descriptive material. The process for FMP adoption after Council development requires nearly one year.

- Possible objectives... are "bare minimum" objectives in that most of the data required for their choice is required under the need for FMPs to "describe the fishery." Even these objectives are far from simple.

- Much of the information required by law for FMP development does not exist. (The council in the 1990s was sued by a conservation group for its failure to prepare a skate plan. The council had been delayed in its effort to prepare the plan because information required by law did not exist.)

The report by Development Sciences noted that the National Standards, spelled out in MFCMA and to which all management plans must conform, must be interpreted *before* objectives are chosen to achieve them. In other words, the council was confronted with a circular process; it couldn't choose objectives until it had defined the standards that would constrain the objectives.

The report from Development Sciences (Anon. MS 1977:5) stated that the following terms were not defined by MFCMA; *Optimum Yield, Overfishing, Efficiency, Capacity.* It went on to point out that:

> If only one FMP were needed to manage the FCZ, these terms would require definition once. As it is, however, a lack of information about how marine fisheries stocks are interrelated forces FMP development largely on a species-by-species basis. These terms would *require different definition for each FMP*; those definitions would have to be consistent with each other (emphasis added).

MFCMA refers to "maximum sustainable yield" and requires that MSY be considered in determining OY. But, according to senior NMFS scientists,

> Regrettably from the point of view of practical management this model [MSY] does not describe what often happens in nature. It assumes that the young added to a population are proportional to the numbers of adults, while practical experience with most fish populations has shown this to be untrue (Hennemuth et al. 1980:5).

At the same time Larkin (1980:256) stated that "In many fisheries of the world it is simply not realistic to pursue the objective of maximum sustainable yield of a particular stock of a particular species."

Thus the council was in the position of having not one unequivocal, objective, firmly fixed point of departure for managing fish stocks. Every important standard and definition was, in fact, undefined, vague, left to the councils to clarify, and subject to differing judgments - and, because of that, sooner or later to litigation.

Time delays

Why did it take nearly three years to implement the Interim Plan, intended to be simple, quickly implemented, and non-controversial? Why did it take nearly six years to develop the Atlantic Demersal Finfish (ADF) plan, only then to have it partially disapproved by NMFS and then partially implemented a year later? Part of the answer is the "incredibly complex and cumbersome process for FMP adoption" (Anon. MS 1977:35), but compliance with the various time-consuming administrative steps is only a small part of the answer. Weber (2002:177) noted another reason: "When the councils began preparing fishery management plans and the NMFS began reviewing them, the councils and the agency found that much of the federal research conducted over the previous several decades did not answer the kinds of questions that fisheries managers were confronting." This lack of answers to key management questions reflects the general lack of practical management experience prior to MFCMA. But the principal reasons for the council difficulties were the complexities of the fisheries themselves. The council in its groundfish plan had to deal simultaneously with:

1) a variety of intermixed species, each of differing distributional and migratory patterns and of differing conditions of biomass;

2) the diversity of fishing gear used to catch the species;

3) the problems inherent in the otter trawl, the principal method of catching groundfish;

4) the problems it had learned by hard experience that arise from quotas, seasonal allocations, and trip limits;

5) differing objectives within the fishing industry for the various stocks; and

6) the lack of clear and generally accepted objectives or purposes of management.

It had to deal with the impact of its proposed ADF regulations upon fisheries that were not included in ADF and that did not need the stringent management required by the species included in ADF - because every proposed regulation of ADF had an impact upon other fisheries. And the council could not devote its full attention to those complexities; at the same time it was trying to develop plans for other species such as herring and scallops that were not directly (but certainly indirectly) related to the groundfish problems, but that were also complicated and equally controversial.

A complex fishery

As early as June 1978 the Acting Administrator of the National Oceanic and Atmospheric Administration, the parent agency of NMFS, wrote to the chairman of the New England council: [28]

> Three factors have made it extremely difficult to stabilize this [groundfish] fishery, conserve its resources, and prevent economic harm to the fishermen since the plan was put into effect: 1) the substantial influx of new vessels and fishing capacity; 2) a lack of agreement about the

---

[28] James P. Walsh to Edward J. MacLeod, June 28, 1978.

objectives of the plan [not surprising since the original plan prepared by NMFS stated none]; and 3) continuing uncertainty because of repeated changes in regulations. Unfortunately, we seem to be in a constant state of crisis, unable to come to grips with the basic question of the best management objectives for the fishery.

One might think that listing all these problems is simply a self-serving excuse for not making the "hard decisions" needed to conserve groundfish; that managing groundfish is really a simple business if only one has the will to do it. One wishes that were so. That it is not so can be verified by referring to the requirements of the MFCMA. One provision is that management plans shall not discriminate among fishermen. [29] The fact that migrating fish appear in different areas in different months means that annual or quarterly quotas almost certainly will adversely affect - or discriminate against - fishermen of some areas. Some groundfish are available to some fishermen in some areas, but only later to fishermen in other areas. Thus the fishermen of eastern Maine or the mid-Atlantic region may find that the annual or quarterly quota for codfish has been taken and the fishery closed before the fish appeared in their area. Such in fact was the case in 1978 when the annual cod quota was taken before the fish appeared in eastern Maine. The plan has clearly discriminated against them; they are excluded from the fishery by the quotas. Indeed, the groundfish fishery in eastern Maine in 2008 is practically extinct.

The council considered closing certain areas thought to be important to successful spawning of groundfish. But fish species

---

[29] National Standard 4 states that "Conservation and management measures shall not discriminate between residents of different states. If it becomes necessary to allocate or assign fishing privileges among various United States fishermen, such allocation shall be (A) fair and equitable to all such fishermen; (B) reasonably calculated to promote conservation; and (C) carried out in such manner that no particular individual, corporation, or other entity acquires an excessive share of such privileges."

and fish stocks are not neatly separated into distinct, non-overlapping areas of distribution; there is much overlap in their distributions. This of course means that if an area is closed to otter-trawl fishing for spawning cod, then in effect it is closed to all species, and fishermen who are looking for other species and who are not interested in cod cannot fish in the closed areas. This reduces the options that fishermen have for responding to natural variations in the numbers of various species. It limits their ability to shift from one species to another, as they have traditionally done for generations, as species naturally fluctuate in numbers or distributions. A mesh regulation intended to protect juvenile and immature cod or haddock may preclude fishing for other species that require a different mesh size and are not included in ADF.

The Task Force

The Northeast Fisheries Management Task Force was created in 1979 on the initiative of a senior NMFS scientist, Brian Rothschild, specifically to assist NEFMC in developing a better groundfish management plan. It was composed of representatives of NMFS, academia, the fishing industry, and the New England and Mid-Atlantic councils, people with undoubted expertise in fisheries science and practical experience in the fisheries. We will refer to it frequently throughout this work as The Task Force. Its report to the council included discussion of the mixed nature of the fisheries. The Task Force (Hennemuth et al. 1980:3,7) noted that in general

> in a multispecies fishery, for example, management concentrating upon one or two principal species and ignoring the complex of species making up the bycatch may indeed approach optimal catch levels for the species selected but in so doing reduce catches for the fishery as a whole to suboptimal levels....Preoccupation with "target" species of a fishery, without due attention to the effect of management on the fishes composing the bycatch, could lead to unplanned-for, and possibly adverse effects on the condition of the bycatch stocks....There is another kind of

interaction between species at the harvesting level. Fishermen switch their effort from species to species seasonally and according to abundance and price, in order to maximize their profits. Managers must be alert to the effect that regulatory measures directed at one species may have upon this seasonal switching by fishermen and upon their annual income.

This became a significant difficulty in the development of the Interim Plan, as it did with ADF, and could in any management plan. The council intended to provide protection within that plan to spawning codfish by means of closed areas and to juvenile codfish by means of a specified mesh size. But both of those protective measures in effect prohibited a fishery for silver hake, for example, from large parts of the Gulf of Maine. The council therefore took great pains to develop the Exempted Fisheries Program by which, under certain conditions, fishermen could target species with smaller meshes and in the protected areas. [30] The council proposed nine specific conditions for participation in the Exempted Fisheries Program, some of which immediately provoked criticisms from within the council, from NMFS, and from the fishing industry. An interesting industry objection was that the Interim Plan (and the groundfish plan of 1977, for that matter) did not give the council the authority to regulate any species not specifically designated for conservation management within that plan. The argument was that if the council intended to regulate small-mesh fisheries, as in fact was the intent of the Exempted Fisheries Program, then under the law it would have to develop a full fisheries management plan, with all the require-ments and time constraints of the law included in the plan. There is validity in the legal sense to this position, but clearly it would nullify the basic purposes - timeliness and simplicity - of the Interim Plan. The only way out of this legal dilemma was for the council to ignore it, which it did. The industry also noted that the

---

[30] The initial list of "small mesh" fisheries included silver hake, redfish, squid, northern shrimp, and dogfish. Later, red hake, herring, mackerel, and ocean pout were considered.

Exempted Fisheries Program would induce fishermen to falsify their logbooks to avoid violations and maintain their eligibility for the small-mesh option. This, too, would nullify one of the purposes of the Interim Plan - to improve the reliability of the landings data by eliminating quotas and the incentives for false reports created by quotas.

The council was at pains to develop a workable small-mesh fishery program because it recognized that if its measures to protect cod, haddock, and yellowtail flounder precluded fisheries for other species, then those fishermen would of necessity focus on the regulated species and further add to fishing mortality on them and to the problem of reducing the mortalities of those species.

Uncertain purposes

Adding equally to the complications and delays in implementing the Interim Plan was the "fail-safe" concern. It was based on a fear held by a number of council members that the IP, consisting of only minimal and indirect conservation measures, would stimulate an "open" fishery and lead to serious stock declines. But there was no obvious scientific measure or consensus within the council or NMFS of what would constitute a "serious" decline or what should be done about it if it should occur. The extended debate, over a period of several council meetings and several months, included discussion of whether a "serious" problem should include economic as well as biological issues. In fact the council was unable to quantify what it meant by a serious problem.

These complications had not been anticipated by the original proponents of the Interim Plan, and they became a significant cause of delay in implementation of the plan. Indeed, they were potentially serious departures from the primary and most important objective of the original proposal; that is, to devise as simple and non-controversial a plan as possible with the primary purpose of eliminating the many problems that arose from the original plan and, most importantly, to give the council the time and opportunity to deliberate carefully on the content and purpose of the new groundfish plan, ADF, - without the constant interruptions and crises that had consumed its energies and credibility since June 1977.

Unintended consequences - again

The council was well aware that any form of quota or trip limit led to "high-grading," the practice of throwing away fish of lesser value and landing, within the quota or trip limit, only the fish of highest value. They could also lead to "split trips" in which a vessel might land part of its catch at a port in which a fish buyer might be less than scrupulous in recording the landing, and landing the legal part of its catch in its home port where it would be recorded against the trip limit or quota.

By hard experience the council had learned that it had to anticipate all the unintended consequences of its proposed regulations. It is for this reason that the council and its committees and its staff and advisors spent many hours thoroughly debating not only the hoped-for benefits of any proposal, but also the probable negative aspects of each proposal. The council had to consider not only those unwanted consequences of which it had already become aware, but also try to anticipate problems that it had not yet encountered and that very likely would arise as a result of its proposals. It always had to ask "What if?" and to devise, if it could, a response to the "what ifs." And it tried to find solutions within two of its fundamental guiding principles; to avoid prolonged seasonal closures if at all possible, and to disrupt the traditional structure and practices of the New England fishery as little as possible.

A basic purpose

We feel strongly that from the beginning it was a widely held, if unspoken, council philosophy that it was very important for social reasons to try to preserve the traditional structure of the New

England fisheries based largely on family-owned vessels with the capability of switching among species in response to *natural* variabilities in stock numbers. Indeed, in the development of its ADF plan, the council was explicit [31] that 1) the council desired "to avoid socially or economically disruptive changes in the traditional relative shares of various vessel-gear groups in the fisheries for regulated species," and 2) "freedom of decision-making and choice for individual participants in the fishery should be maintained to the greatest possible extent."

A hint of fisheries systems

The original groundfish plan of 1977 included only three species. Two years later, when the council decided that it must develop a wholly new management plan, ADF, it realized the "need for simultaneous determination of management regulations for all groundfish species which as a combined resource complex form the major source of incomes and benefits to the New England and Mid-Atlantic otter trawl and fixed gear fleets as well as to recreational user-groups." [32] The new plan would initially include fifteen species, with the recognition that additional species would have to be included subsequently. The expanded number of species was necessary because of 1) biological interdependencies of the species and 2) economic interactions among them. Analysis by the council staff [33] "provides evidence of the high degree of interaction within demersal finfish fisheries." Thus the council concluded "that species which to a large extent are harvested

---

[31] reported by Guy Marchessault, Richard Ruais, and Der-Hsiung Wang: History & Status of the Atlantic Demersal Finfish Fishery Management Plan: a Report for the Northeast Fisheries Management Task Force. Undated MS.

[32] Fishery Management Plan for the Atlantic Groundfish Fishery. Part 1: Statement of the Problem. NEFMC staff. Res.Doc. 79 GF 4.2. April, 1979

[33] Marchessault, Ruais, Wang: ibid.

jointly and/or individually contribute in a seasonal pattern to the earnings of the mobile and fixed-gear groundfish fleets should form part of the resource complex of an Atlantic Groundfish FMP."

David Pierce, in his summary of the evolution of the groundfish plan (MS 1982:71), gave hypothetical examples of the biological and economic linkages among the various species:

Assume a fisherman went fishing with a small mesh net for whiting. His first tow yielded 5,000 lbs. whiting, 3,000 lbs. winter flounder, and 2,000 lbs. cod... The second tow plus poundage of the first gave him 10,000 lbs. whiting, 5,000 lbs. winter flounder, 2,000 lbs. dabs [plaice], and 3,000 lbs. cod." Thus four species typically were part of normal fishing operations, and they all contributed to the fisherman's income. In the original plan one of them (cod) was subject to stringent regulations, but the others were not. The status of the regulated species could and did seriously affect the fishermen's' ability to harvest non-regulated species that contributed significantly to their income.

Multiple jurisdictions

Further contributing to the council's difficulties was the matter of multiple management jurisdictions. Not all of the fifteen species determined to be included in ADF, because of their significant interdependencies, lay entirely or primarily within the New England Council's jurisdiction. The Mid-Atlantic Council had primary jurisdiction over and was developing plans for several of the species. This situation created the necessity for simultaneous determination by the two councils of the management regulations for these species, assuming the two councils concurred in the need for and the kind of regulations and the objectives to be achieved by those regulations. And no groundfish species lay wholly within the Fishery Conservation Zone, the area of the council's jurisdiction and authority. Seven states (Maine through New Jersey) and Canada had management jurisdiction in varying degrees over groundfish species whose ranges included coastal waters inside the FCZ. The council could not dictate management policy to those entities; it could only hope to persuade them to adopt compatible management practices - and with Canada not directly, but only fourth-hand through diplomatic intermediaries. The Canadian issue was partially addressed by the U.S.-Canadian Fisheries Agreement negotiated in 1979 that assigned management responsibilities and national shares for specified fish stocks. It established three categories of fish stocks, each category of fish to be managed on a different basis. Category A included transboundary stocks, such as pollock and cusk, that were to be subject to joint management by a U.S.-Canadian Fisheries Commission. Category B species included *some* cod and haddock, and three species of hakes. These species were subject to joint management based on proposals to the commission submitted by the country with assigned primary management responsibility. Category C species included Gulf of Maine cod and redfish. For these species, the joint Commission served as a forum for consultation only on management measures proposed by the country having management responsibility. The coastal states thus would manage these stocks but consultation was required prior to implementation of management measures.

Without considering the effectiveness of this complicated management agreement between the two countries, this brief outline serves the purpose of illustrating the problems of management inherent in the varying distributions of the several species under multiple management jurisdictions.

Finally, to further add to the complications of managing New England groundfish, the NEFMC staff report [34] to The Task Force noted that the ADF "management measures and regulations will also be sensitive to the impact on fisheries other than those included in the ADF FMP." But the staff's report did not elaborate on that note.

---

[34] Marchessault, Ruais, Wang: ibid.

Critics may protest that all of this apparent complexity could have been dealt with by a hard-nosed, resolute council decision to close a fishery when a quota had been reached. Simple and effective. But, again, a decision to close the hard-pressed haddock fishery, for example, meant diversion of effort into the cod fishery. Or a closure of both meant diversion of effort into the "small-mesh" fisheries for whiting, for example, which inevitably resulted in unreported and discarded catches of cod and haddock. Followed to its logical conclusion, a closure meant no groundfish fishing at all, with all the economic consequences throughout coastal New England. Critics note that New England has lost tens of millions of dollars and hundreds of jobs from depleted fish stocks and ineffective management. They do not note that a fishery closure could mean the loss of *all* the groundfishing-related jobs in the region. And they do not note the ripple effect upon other fisheries. The service industries supported by income from groundfishing vessels also support scallop, lobster, herring and other fisheries; without groundfish income those services could be forced to close, depriving the other fisheries of their services.

Perhaps a limited-entry program would have solved the problem. This is a common perception. NMFS urged the concept upon the council, but NMFS never proposed or suggested a specific plan for limited entry appropriate for the New England fisheries that would have dealt with the numerous problems inherent in such a proposal that were evident to council members. And such a plan would not have dealt with problems inherent in the overlapping distributions of a variety of species that required different meshes in otter trawls.

This review of problems with which the council was faced may appear complex and bewildering - as indeed it did at the time to the council which for years struggled with the problems and looked for solutions (Recall that in March 1981 the NMFS Regional Administrator had also recognized that "there may not be a solution to the groundfish management situation"). But perhaps with hindsight the complications can be categorized and simplified somewhat. In trying to simplify and clarify these problems, we put aside the issues arising from the administrative requirements built into, or added on to, MFCMA, and the uncertain and contentious relations between NEFMC and NMFS. We view these issues more as nuisance factors than as fundamental problems of management. They are real problems, but they could be mitigated by congressional clarification and simplification of its intent as to the council's authority for management and administrative procedures.

Three critical issues

We focus here on what we believe are three basic management problems that would prevail under *any* management system or regime. One immediate inference is that much of the complexity and difficulties that frustrated the council are a consequence of the kind of gear that is the otter trawl. It would appear that in fact there is no solution to a number of problems faced by the council as long as the otter trawl is the principal harvesting gear. Those problems include:

-   unavoidable and substantial bycatches of a variety of species

-   the fact that the otter trawl in a single tow may unavoidably catch more of a regulated species than is legal, with the necessity to discard - probably injured or dead - the excess catch;

-   the fact that no single mesh size is appropriate for all species that may be taken;

-   the fact that there is unavoidable scale damage and perhaps fatal injury and unquantified mortality to fishes that pass through the meshes of nets;

-   imperfect selectivity between juveniles and adults of any species; and

-   possible damage to the bottom habitat and bottom-living

creatures.

The only solution to those problems would come from developing a new harvesting concept that does not embody the inherent problems of the otter trawl, a possibility we shall consider below.

A second inference is that the council could not effectively control fishing effort or fishing mortality with the traditional tactics. Neither the Coast Guard nor NMFS had the capability to enforce the regulations. There is a perception that the council, under pressure from the industry, chose by its Interim Plan to permit unlimited freedom of fishing without constraints. Such is not the case. Even after IP was adopted, the council continued to search for effective methods of controlling fishing effort and fish mortalities. The council did consider, in varying degrees of depth, the various options for effort or mortality control as they were then known and understood. Each had at least some advocates within the council, but none could be seen to be both applicable and sufficiently effective with New England's complex groundfish fishery. And all were seen to have unintended consequences upon the other fisheries of the region. This should suggest that, like harvesting gear, new concepts are needed for effective control of effort and mortalities in these complex fisheries.

Finally, the number of species included in the groundfish plan inevitably increased as the council was forced to take into account the inextricable but often undefined or unquantified inter-relationships - biological and economic - among those species. In 1976 NMFS had told the council that it would have to manage *fifty*-odd species, each with its own, *separate*, management plan. Neither the NMFS advice nor the incremental addition of species to the council plan explicitly recognized the possibility that the fishes of New England might be part of a *system* - an ecosystem - with the implication that a plan to manage a system might be easier and more effective than attempting to deal with a dozen or several dozen species with no clear idea of the critical biological interactions among them. There was increasing talk in this period of holistic or multispecies or ecosystems management of fishes, but nothing was done about it.

We will consider these three issues - 1) fishing technologies, 2) effort controls, and 3) ecosystems management - in detail later in this discussion. We believe that they are at the heart of the continuing problems of groundfish management.

6) Origin and Structure of the Councils

We should note first that this chapter is based to a considerable degree upon a two-day conversation held in September 2004 among seven persons, [35] six of whom were directly involved, either as congressional staff or counsel to the staffs or as industry lobbyists, in the drafting of the original MFCMA. They have all been actively engaged with the fishing industry and MFCMA ever since. There was general agreement among them concerning the evolution of the legislation and of the congressional intent behind it.

The gathering storm

Following World War Two European nations greatly enlarged their fishing operations to supply much-needed protein for their populations, many of whom were suffering from years of malnutrition. Their fishing fleets had been reduced during the war, and to replace them and to support expanded fisheries they developed a new class of fishing and processing vessels, very large factory-trawlers, that had the capability to fish anywhere in the world. They adopted the latest electronic technologies, much of which, such as sonar, was developed during the war. The northwest Atlantic with its rich fishing grounds on the Grand Banks off Newfoundland was particularly attractive to them. And within a few years the vessels were fishing in areas where they had never fished before. "In the two decades following World WarTwo, the world fish catch increased over 300%" (Alverson 2002:5).

---

[35] The participants were Dayton L Alverson, George Mannina, Rod Moore, Richard Sharood, Lucy Sloan, and the authors.

In response to the greatly increased fishing effort in the northwest Atlantic, the United Sates and Canada in the late 1940s urged international agreements for the conservation and management of fish stocks off their shores. The International Commission for the Northwest Atlantic Fisheries (ICNAF) was formed in 1950 by eleven countries (eventually there were eighteen signatory nations) and it immediately began a program of stock assessments and the formulation of management recommendations and regulations.

In the 1950s and 1960s vessels from Japan, Bulgaria, Poland, Cuba and other countries not originally part of ICNAF arrived on the fishing grounds off Newfoundland and Nova Scotia, and in 1961 sixty-one factory-trawlers from the Soviet Union, operating as coordinated fleets, suddenly appeared on Georges Bank and Nantucket Shoals off New England. They were soon joined by other fishing nations. In August 1963 nearly 300 Soviet vessels fished on Georges Bank. Their appearance immediately aroused great concern in the New England fishing industry and among government fisheries officials.

> From 1965 to 1969, the peak harvest year, the U.S. fishing fleet landed an estimated 723,000 metric tons of cod, haddock, and yellowtail flounder from the fishing grounds of Georges Bank, southern New England, and the Gulf of Maine. The foreign fleets caught and processed almost *sixteen* times that amount from the same waters. New England landings for these same species soon began to decline. In New Bedford, where yellowtail flounder and scallops made up the bulk of the catch, yellowtail flounder landings fell from 34,700 metric tons in 1965 to 17,000 metric tons in 1976. The percentage of haddock landed from Georges Bank by U.S. fishermen dropped from 90 percent in 1960 to slightly more than 10 percent in 1972. The rest was taken by foreign vessels. Gulf of Maine cod landings dropped from 92 million pounds to 41 million pounds (emphasis added) (Playfair 2002:32).

Even before the arrival of foreign fleets off New England there had been general concern that the fisheries of the United States were only sixth in size compared to other fishing nations, and that the United States fishing fleet was inefficient and under-developed. This perception was the primary motivation for federal government policy, including the Capital Construction Fund and the Fishing Vessel Obligation Guarantee Program, in the late 1960s and early 1970s. The report in 1969 of the Stratton Commission, which was established by Congress to study and make recommendations about the entire United States ocean policy, concluded that "The goal of domestic fisheries manage-ment must be the development of a technically advanced and economically efficient fishing fleet with the minimum number of units required to take the catch over a prolonged period of time" (Commission on Marine Science, Engineering and Resources 1969:93). This proposed policy rested upon estimates at the time that global, sustainable marine fish yields could reach as high as 2000 million metric tons per year. The commission stated (1969:88), "It is... realistic to expect total annual production of marine food products... to grow between 400 and 500 million mt annually, before expansion costs become excessive". The Stratton Commission intended that the United States fishing industry should have its share of that expanding catch. The commission's forecast was made at the time when the total world fish landings were about 60 million mt. They have not exceeded about 90 million mt at any time since [36] (although in addition there may be an unrecorded bycatch of about 29 million tons (Alverson et al. 1994)).

The New England fishing industry, particularly, had not experienced the growth and modernization of its fleet after the World War Two as had the European and other fleets. The

---

[36] John Gulland (1972), in contrast to optimistic forecasts, had estimated that the potential sustainable yield from traditional fisheries resources was about 100 million tons, with a practical limit of about 80 million tons.

majority of the New England vessels were small, old, and not efficient in the fish-catching sense as were the European vessels. "Seventy-five percent of the boats in Gloucester were over twenty years old, run-down, and outmoded, according to Manuel Lewis of the Gloucester Fisheries Commission" (Dewar 1983:111). The development of the New England fleet was limited in part by the fact of a limited domestic market; fish at that time was not a popular item in the American diet.

The negotiations within ICNAF after some years resulted in setting minimum mesh sizes for otter trawls and catch allocations among nations within overall allowable quotas for various species. But questions of compliance and enforcement among a diversity of nations fishing with a variety of motives and objectives were always present. Compliance varied among nations, and enforcement depended upon the cooperation of the parties to ICNAF. And the pace of ICNAF progress in conservation was considered much too slow by the New England fishing industry. Indeed, by the mid 1960s record numbers of haddock were taken by Soviet vessels on Georges Bank. Haddock landings by all nations exceed 250,000 tons and the stock then began a precipitous decline to record low numbers in 1974 from which the stock had not recovered thirty years later.

New England fishermen began a campaign to persuade Congress to extend U.S. fisheries jurisdiction to 200 miles from shore, primarily to control or eliminate foreign fishing vessels that were taking extraordinary quantities of fish and with which the New England vessels could not compete. In fact, years earlier President Truman had declared that in special cases the United States had the right to establish conservation zones offshore, beyond the three-mile Territorial Sea, to protect threatened species.

The Truman proclamation had become an accepted tenet of international law by 1958. In that year, the International Conference on the Law of the Sea concluded a Convention on Fishing and Conservation of the Living Resources of the High Seas, which proclaimed that coastal nations have a "special interest in the maintenance of the productivity of the living resources in any area of the high seas adjacent to [their] territorial sea[s" (Bean and Rowland 1997:149).

In 1966 the United States did extend its fisheries jurisdiction from three miles to twelve miles offshore. But this tentative measure was too little and too late.

At the same time that very large numbers of fish were taken by the factory trawlers off Canadian shores and particularly off New England, in the 1960s and early 1970s, large vessels had also voyaged to previously unexploited fishing grounds off Africa and the coasts of other underdeveloped countries. The same kinds of concerns raised in New England were increasingly voiced by the governments of countries off which the new fleets fished because of the perceived threat to the development of their own domestic fisheries. As a result in part of the increasing concerns of underdeveloped countries, the United Nations initiated a series of Law of the Sea (LOS) Conferences. The conferences would consider not just fisheries but also oil exploration in the sea, deep-sea ocean mining, freedom-of-navigation issues, the legal limits to the width of territorial seas, and other maritime issues. The developments and problems in these diverse areas of concern since the World War Two have been called "the gathering storm" by Lee Alverson who participated in the LOS conferences; they would precipitate all subsequent events for world-wide marine fisheries management.

In the series of LOS conferences, there was growing momentum for declarations of extended fisheries jurisdictions to 200 miles offshore, primarily from underdeveloped countries that wished to preserve their resources from foreign fishing fleets and develop their own fisheries. That policy was vigorously opposed by the United States administration and by other developed countries for a number of reasons. The United States Navy and State Department wished to preserve maximum freedom of navigation. The U.S. high-seas tuna and shrimp industries which fished off foreign shores were opposed. The U.S. oil and mining industries and their government representatives wished to preserve access to mineral resources on and beneath the continental shelves and in deeper water around the world.

Congressional action

In spite of these powerful forces in opposition, early in the 1970s the fishing industries of Alaska and New England were able to get congressional sponsors for extended jurisdiction legislation. As it became increasingly clear that relief for the fishing industry was not to be expected in the foreseeable future from ICNAF or the LOS conferences, congressional support grew for extended jurisdiction even though administration opposition continued and remained strong. The prospects for congressional enactment were increased when the proposed legislation was expanded, with support from Alaska but not New England, to include authority for management of domestic fisheries in addition to simple extended jurisdiction. The congressional supporters became persuaded that in view of administration opposition it was not possible to enact extended jurisdiction by itself without a specific directive for domestic management. And so the prospect of domestic management within extended jurisdiction became a powerful element in the congressional debates.

Within the LOS deliberations, meanwhile, the concepts of MSY and OY had emerged as management justifications for extended jurisdiction. The concept of OY, which included economic and social as well as biological considerations, attained importance in the LOS negotiations because many advocates of management believed at that time that economic objectives could be of greater importance than purely biological considerations; thus OY permitted greater flexibility in management. The underdeveloped countries, particularly, advocated OY as supporting their social and economic agendas. And because they had minimal or weak fisheries science capabilities, OY better served their purposes than the science-based concept of MSY. In spite of the slow pace of the LOS conferences, it became apparent that there was world-wide movement - apparently an inevitability - toward extended fisheries jurisdiction, toward world-wide 200-mile zones.

With this reality emerging, congressional support increased for unilateral U.S. action. It was reinforced by "newly formed marine conservation groups... along with the nationwide organizations of the environmental movement such as the Sierra Club, Friends of the Earth, and the National Wildlife Federation" (Dewar 1983:136). The focus of the battle in Congress subtly shifted from simple extended jurisdiction itself, now nearly a certainty, to the conditions and structure for management. George Mannina, a participant in the drafting negotiations, recalled that while it was sound politics to focus on the problem of foreign fishing and minimize the role of science, "the big elephant in the room was with the management of domestic fisheries." Some industry advisors to the U.S. delegation at LOS conferences, seeing the writing on the wall, had begun to discuss the organization and nature of management under extended jurisdiction; they drafted a number of principles or standards as a basis for management. And a senior administration official handed a congressional staff person a set of management principles to be included in the legislation. But industry advocates who lobbied just for extended jurisdiction alone were taken by surprise when the management provisions appeared in legislation quite late in the congressional drafting process.

Although most industry spokesmen declared that they thought domestic fishery management might be necessary, a National Marine Fisheries Service survey showed that they did not like the proposals they saw. They opposed every specific suggestion about how management might work. Fishing spokesmen were caught in a bind. They played up the devastation of the fish resources and emphasized the conservation aspects of excluding foreigners in order to attract the backing of environmental groups and congressmen sensitive to environmental issues. They would have jeopardized that support if they had openly opposed controls on domestic fishermen, but their fishery constituents did not want management. If the spokesmen could just persuade Congress to pass legislation to exclude foreigners first, they could fight bills to manage American fishermen (Dewar 1983:137-8).

But Dykstra, a spokesman for the industry who attended every drafting session for the legislation, recalls no industry intent to "fight bills to manage American fishermen." Rather, the industry was persuaded that the American fleet did not then have the capacity to damage the stocks which, fishermen believed, would surely recover with the removal of foreign fleets. And so the industry was not concerned or worried about - did not anticipate - the possibility of stringent domestic conservation or management.

There were several critical elements within the management debate. The most important was who - which agency - was to have management authority. One participant in the House drafting process, Richard Sharood, tried hard to spell out the details for management options and authority, but Senate staff were not receptive and did not take this issue seriously, thinking that because NMFS would of course control management, or at least make the critical decisions, such details were unnecessary. But there was intense industry opposition, principally from Alaska, to NMFS management. The federal government had previously had limited experience in domestic fisheries management and most of that had concerned salmon in Alaska. There the perception was that the federal management had not gone well. Because of that, the representatives from the Pacific Northwest in particular did not want federal management of the fisheries. As an alternative, the Alaskans proposed that the legislation provide for regional councils similar to salmon commissions, which included industry representatives, that had been formed in the Pacific Northwest. Elsewhere, also, and particularly in New England, there was industry distrust of the possibility of management by the federal government. And there was general antipathy to the principle of centralized management of the nation's regional and diverse fisheries. In fact, according to George Mannina, there was "huge tension - it became a huge, time-consuming issue" over the question of NMFS management versus a regional council structure. The congressional Eastland Survey in the early 1970s concerning the status of the fishing industry had emphasized the regional nature of the fisheries which contributed to the arguments for regional councils. Opposition to the proposal for council management was in part because of a belief that it would put fishing industry people, who presumably had no technical management expertise, in charge - that non-scientists would run the system. The scientific community was generally hostile to such a possibility.

The congressional staffs received no help from NMFS or the administration in drafting the legislation; when the staffs asked for assistance from NMFS, there was little response. NMFS prohibited its Regional Administrators from participating in the drafting. Participants in the drafting process believe this was because NMFS assumed the legislation would not be passed by Congress or would be vetoed by the president.

NMFS officials in Washington were accustomed to controlling fishery management because they had served as commissioners or as influential advisors to ICNAF....NMFS officials had fought hard to cement their management authority in the new legislation. Although they lost the battle, they continued to believe that the authority was rightfully theirs and that they were more qualified to make decisions than the councils. Officials at the State Department had kept the authority to make final decisions about foreign fishing....Conflict over fishery management among the councils, the National Marine Fisheries Service, and the State Department was inevitable (Dewar 1983:146).

There was opposition, also, to the proposal for management by regional councils based on the perception that councils would include interest-conflicted industry representatives. When drafting the sections of MFCMA concerning the structure of regional councils, the question of conflict of interest among fishing industry representatives on the councils was addressed. After extensive staff debates, the staff report specifically stated that such participation would be essential because of their expert knowledge of the diverse fisheries and would *not* constitute a conflict. But Margaret Dewar (1983:144) commented that "Fishery management could become indulgent self-regulation unless groups with other interests, environmentalist or consumers, for example, became involved."

In the end, of course, MFCMA provided for regional councils, in part at least perhaps because Congress and the administration knew that fisheries management would unavoidably be contentious and controversial. They therefore were content to let the councils take the heat and be buffers between the industry and the federal government. As it turned out, only a minority of the eight councils created by MFCMA wanted the responsibility of management.

The legislation in its final form had three purposes: 1) "Americanization" of the fisheries off the U.S. shores (i. e., removal foreign fishing vessels); 2) development of the U.S. fishing industry; and 3) conservation and management of the domestic fisheries. Congress viewed these as of equal importance but as immediate and future priorities. The first purpose was rather quickly achieved; in just a few years foreign fishing vessels were gone from U.S. waters. Because of the general concern by the administration about the underdeveloped state of the U.S. fisheries and because of the recommendations of the Stratton Commission of 1969 for the "modernization" of the U.S. fleet, development was then considered to be the primary goal. The Stratton Commission used the term "management" in the sense of development of the industry, not conservation of fish. Conservation, according to the commission report, was to be achieved primarily by removing the foreign fleets and foreign competition. Apparently the drafters of MFCMA did not believe that the U.S. fleet had the capacity to overfish, reflected in part by the absence of a definition of overfishing in the legislation. But Congress saw the possible need as a priority in the future for active management for resource conservation itself as the U.S.

fleet increased its capacity and efficiency. MFCMA was intended to be a framework within which possible resource problems in the future could be addressed. There apparently was general recognition that, because there was very limited domestic management experience, the conservation and management provisions of the legislation were experimental to a high degree and that modifications and revisions might be necessary to accomplish all the congressional intent.

The concepts of MSY and OY were included as part of the public relations effort deemed desirable or even necessary to enact the legislation, but they were not precisely defined. Even though the concepts, both MSY and OY, were then considered to be the state of the art, no one knew how to enforce a system based on MSY or OY. ICNAF had not included MSY in its management measures because the commission had no concept for its practical application. With practical management experience since 1976, the vague concepts of MSY and OY now seem rather naive. Overfishing could have been defined in terms of the technical concepts of "recruitment" or "growth" overfishing. Apparently, however, there was in the early 1970s no consensus among scientists on a definition of overfishing, and so overfishing like other critical terms in the legislation, such as MSY, was left vague. [37] This was deliberate. As George Mannina recalled, the general feeling seemed to be that "experience will teach us how to define them."

The nature of the Act

MFCMA has been characterized (Bean 1983:384) thus: "In the degree of planning it requires and in the mechanisms it establishes for the accomplishment of its goals, the Act introduces wholly

---

[37] Dr. Robert M. White, Administrator of NOAA, chaired a fisheries study committee in the 1970s on which the directors of NMFS science centers served. Even with such specialists participating, its report did not define overfishing.

new ideas not found elsewhere in the body of federal wildlife law." A principal congressional sponsor of the act acknowledged to a staff member that it was an experiment; if it doesn't work it would be changed either by appropriate modifications or by abolishing the councils. George Mannina recalled that the congressman's view reflected a general recognition that the legislation embarked upon a new paradigm in fisheries management and no one knew for certain what direction it would take.

Underlying these uncertainties was what one participant in our September 2004 discussion, Lee Alverson, called the "pretty primitive state of knowledge of population dynamics in 1976." This observation may benefit from hindsight twenty-eight years later, but the reality, according to Alverson, is that at that time no one had any idea of MSY, upon which management plans were to be based, for any Pacific coast species and the best guess was that it would take twenty to thirty years to develop those estimates.

In the absence of strict or commonly-agreed-upon definitions of critical terms, Congress left it to the councils to define the terms based upon their knowledge of the characteristics of their regional fisheries. But the act included National Standards by which management plans would be evaluated by the Secretary of Commerce, the supervisor of NMFS and NOAA, who had final authority to approve or disapprove management plans. As we noted before, the idea of national standards came out of discussions among industry advisors to U.S. delegations to LOS conferences. Senate staff insisted that such standards be included in the act, and so staff emphasis was how to draft them so that they would in fact be effective. "The Senate report accompanying the original Act described the overfishing prohibition as 'the most basic objective of fishery management.' [But] Twenty years later, Congress was still struggling with how best to prevent overfishing and rebuild depleted stocks" (Bean and Rowland 1997:157). The congressional intent, then, was that because critical terms in the act were vague the councils would have considerable discretion - latitude - in writing management plans, but the plans would be under overall review by the Secretary of Commerce whose approval would be guided by the National Standards [38]. The act thus set the stage for two potentially differing judgments - the council's and the secretary's - to decide upon the acceptability of management plans based upon undefined terms and vague concepts. As it turned out, this was not just a potential problem. We earlier noted the tension between NEFMC and NMFS on the concept of Optimum Yield.

There was no discussion, apparently, in the drafting process of the objectives of management beyond "achieving and maintaining, on a long term basis the optimum yield from each fishery.". Having provided safeguards in the law through the National Standards, Congress was content to let the councils decide such broad policy issues as what constitutes optimum yield according to their best judgment.

In hindsight, people who were directly involved in drafting MFCMA believe that the legislation as originally enacted could have accomplished the purposes of conservation and management. It was intended to be sufficiently broad and flexible to accommodate the diverse fisheries and fisheries objectives of the nation, and it gave council managers the flexibility to use their experience and best judgment to accomplish the general congressional intent. They believe that the problems experienced since 1977 are due to 1) lack of biological knowledge of the stocks, 2) lack of will, and 3) political interference in the process. They believe that more consideration should have been given to the problems, not then apparent, of 1) overcapitalization, 2) the

---

[38] In brief, the National Standards were; 1) prevent overfishing and assure an optimum yield from each fishery, 2) be based on the best scientific information available, 3) provide for the management of individual or interrelated stocks as a unit, 4) not discriminate between residents of different states, 5) consider efficiency, 6) allow for contingencies, and 7) minimize costs. The amendments of 1996 added three more standards; 8) minimize adverse economic impacts on fishing communities, 9) minimize bycatch, and 10) promote the safety of human life at sea (Bean and Rowland 1997:157).

uncertain state of fisheries science, of how fisheries could be better conserved and managed, and 3) society's changing perception of the proper goals of management. Perhaps more analysis of how the act would work regionally should have been done. Lucy Sloan, an industry lobbyist who closely monitored the drafting process, recalled that the congressional staffs knew very well they were drafting a new, experimental, and quite different system for resource management and they made great efforts, given the knowledge of the time, to do it right. Rod Moore, on the House staff at the time and deeply involved with Pacific fisheries since, believes that with that experience he wouldn't change much of MFCMA as it was prior to the amendments of 1996. But one staff member observed that "we were not wise enough to anticipate the future."

In spite of the problems and controversies that have arisen since 1977, those who wrote the act believe that it was good legislation. It certainly accomplished the congressional purposes of removing foreign fishing fleets from waters adjacent to the United States, of "Americanizing" those fisheries resources, and of revitalizing the American fishing fleet. These were immediate issues of congressional concern in the 1970s. Congress also of course recognized a potential need for conservation efforts within the American fishing industry. It was aware that if the American fleet developed the capacity of the foreign fleets there would again be resource problems and a need for resource management, and it provided for a reasonable if experimental structure and process to that end.

The original drafters have mixed views whether subsequent amendments have been generally beneficial. They believe that while some amendments have been useful, others have drastically shifted the original purpose of MFCMA and some have added considerably and to little purpose to the burdens that the councils must bear in developing management plans. One drafter characterized the more recent amendments as a "disaster" and "a litigator's joy," with the result that management policy is now defined not by the congressionally designated managers but largely by the courts.

Margaret Dewar (1983:144) wrote:

> The legacy of the many years of work to limit foreign fishing and to extend fisheries jurisdiction to 200 miles included much more than the law itself. The experience had molded views among industry spokesmen, fishermen, and officials at NMFS and NOAA that promised to affect the industry and fishery policy in the new era.

The council process and accountability

Early in the existence of the New England council, its members received a flow chart that summarized the process governing review and approval of a council plan. In condensed form the chart, unfolded, was about three feet long, or perhaps a little longer. The chart was generally known as *The Horse Blanket*. It was a complicated diagram with many arrows and boxes and feed-back loops, but its complexity only reflected the legally required steps - or perhaps the administration's interpretations of the required steps - from a council vote on a plan until its approval and implementation by the Secretary of Commerce. One knowledgeable federal fisheries official likened it to a digestive track into which nutritious material was introduced at one end and from which bits of fecal material emerged at the other. As noted above, an early advisory report (Anon. MS 1977:c) to the council remarked that "the council must function within a paper nightmare" and, further, that "Fisheries Management Plans (FMPs) require at the very least exhaustive descriptive material....The process for FMP adoption after council development requires nearly one year." It was later noted (Hennemuth et al. 1980:3), but not fully understood by the council or probably by NMFS in 1977, that

> management is in a real sense experimental. Lessons are learned from the process and incorporated in the form of revisions....management may have to be more or less

reactive, incorporating what is learned in the process of management in revisions of technique and perhaps in redefinition of objectives, when experience shows the original definition to have been unsatisfactory....The greater the uncertainty of the system, the more reactive must be the management approach taken, with a proportionately greater need for timely monitoring of events.

But the "paperwork nightmare" and the time-consuming complexities of The Horse Blanket, the council was to learn, and indeed the ever-increasingly restrictive nature of subsequent amendments to MFCMA, make it very difficult to learn from mistakes and make revisions in a timely fashion. The attitude of NMFS generally was that NEFMC could not experiment and thus learn from its inevitable mistakes, but had to produce in ADF and later versions of the groundfish plan a full and complete, once-and-for-all plan for restoration and maintenance of the groundfish stocks. [39] The court also has ruled that each amendment must in itself provide for full restoration and maintenance of the stocks.

The neat arrows and boxes of the horse-blanket chart implied a review process that, regardless of its complexity, was at least well defined and comprehensible. The process in practice was something other than that. (In practice, no one seemed to pay much attention to The Horse Blanket.) The Task Force (Hennemuth et al. 1980:11) concluded that

> Present experience... indicates that flexibility in the develop-ment, amendment, and implementation of management plans must be *increased* if these plans are to be responsive to the dynamic nature of the fisheries. Plans must be responsive to changing stocks and fishery conditions and to the *unforeseen consequences* of the management plans themselves (emphasis added).

---

[39] But the Regional Administrator at one point told the council, much to its surprise, that plan amendments did not have to solve *all* the problems.

The Task Force (Hennemuth et al. 1980:11) noted that in the early days it took a minimum of 250 days to process or amend an FMP after it was submitted to Washington by a council.

The plans must be reviewed each year, and usually the plans cover one year. Amendments are required to extend the plans into subsequent years, and generally, since these amendments involve quotas and optimum yields, they are considered major amendments. *The result is that the councils must prepare such amendments before the effects of the plan currently in force can be known* (emphasis added).

One must understand that most council decisions were made only after much staff analyses and committee and council discussion. [40] The analyses and discussions about this complicated fishery were necessarily extended because plans had to 1) define and achieve management objectives, 2) abide by the National Standards, and, most important, 3) anticipate and avoid unintended consequences. Most of the planning work took place not in council meetings but in committee meetings. The committee meetings were often attended by advisers and by public and industry observers, most of whom participated in the discussions. The meetings may have been day-long in length and perhaps until late at night. There could be many such meetings. One council member chaired about forty meetings of the groundfish committee in a two-year period. In the meetings every conceivable aspect of a management proposal would be discussed, argued, debated, modified, and possibly put out for further analysis by the council staff or by NMFS. Committee findings would then be presented to the full council which often carried the discussion on at length.

The point is that no council proposal was made without full

---

[40] But some important decisions were made, under council protest, in great haste under NMFS insistence that certain inflexible mandated deadlines had to be met.

consideration, as far as possible, of its implications. But this extensive discussion leading up to a council recommendation or decision was not part of the plan sent on for secretarial approval. (Remember that the council could only propose a plan, not implement it.) It would not be practical to include all the considerations underlying a proposal.

At some uncertain point in the future the council would receive a response to its proposal (for example, six weeks later in the fall of 1977). It would be approved, or disapproved, or sent back for further work. But rarely was it clear who made the operational response. Was it in the NMFS Regional Office? Or at the NMFS Science Center in Woods Hole, Massachusetts? Or within NMFS in Washington, D.C., or in NOAA, or in the NOAA General Council office? (Weber (2002:91} claimed that "Both regional and headquarters staff [of NMFS] also had to answer to the leadership of the parent agency, the NOAA. NOAA administrator Richard Frank relied heavily on the advice of a battery of attorneys that required convincing before they approved any action proposed by NMFS.") Or in the Secretary's office? Or outside the Department of Commerce?

The legal requirement for this review process together with varying definitions and interpretations of undefined but critical terms such as "overfishing," "greatest overall benefit," "relevant," and "optimum yield" inevitably lead to misunderstandings, confusion, and confrontations between the council and the federal bureaucracy. By leaving those terms undefined Congress gave the councils great discretion, apparently deliberately, to use their judgments in defining and applying them. But the reviewers' understanding or interpretation of those terms could very well differ substantially from that of the council's. (Indeed, there were differences of opinion on definitions within the New England council itself.) This situation essentially gave the council, which presumably had expert knowledge of the fishery, the responsibility and authority to develop plans based on its judgments, and gave veto power to other authority(ies), with little direct knowledge or experience of the fishery, based, very likely, on different judgments.

And why had the reviewers made the response that came back to the council? Wherever the reviewer abided within the bureaucracy, it is unlikely that the reviewer was fully or even partially aware of the hours of discussion and the many issues considered by the council or its committee in formulating its proposal. Rarely would a reviewer be in a position to fully understand the reasoning leading to a proposal. And because of the usual anonymity of the reviewer, seldom could the council discuss the question directly with a reviewer for the purpose of explaining or clarifying the rationale for its proposal. The process of semi- or fully anonymous reviews might be repeated for any particular proposal that might then become a cycle of proposal and review and proposal...

The point is that there was no clear point of accountability and responsibility for final decision-making. Thus the council felt frustrated that no matter how hard and carefully it might work on a plan or proposal, its best efforts could be second-guessed by someone, somewhere, with partial or imperfect knowledge of the council's considerations and the bases of its judgments. The council felt that it had the responsibility to devise a plan but not the authority to implement it; indeed, that is the fact. In effect, the process meant that the council was not allowed to make mistakes from which it might learn how to improve the management process.

A decision to disapprove a proposal might turn upon one or more of the somewhat vaguely-defined concepts of the MFCMA. The definition of OY, for example, is in the mind of the beholder. Similarly, the act requires that a plan be based upon the "best science available", but what is the best science may also be a matter of opinion. Nor does the act address the possibility that the best science available might not be very good. A remote reviewer may not even be aware that there is not universal agreement upon the definitions of these and other terms contained within the National Standards for plans. The council might legitimately believe that a proposal did meet the National Standards; a reviewer might not. There is no means of arbitrating these differences, and no final point of responsibility for making those decisions.

An alternative management entity

Several of the council members had had cooperative management experience of a different kind within The Atlantic States Marine Fisheries Commission (ASMFC) prior to the enactment of MFCMA. ASMFC had been created by Congress early in the 1940s for the purpose of encouraging cooperative interstate management of coastal fisheries at the time when the federal government had no such authority. Three New England states (Maine, New Hampshire, and Massachusetts) developed a modest management program for northern shrimp, in good part at the request of shrimp fishermen, using the regulatory authority granted to the states through ASMFC by Congress. The regulatory procedures of ASMFC were a stark contrast to those of MFCMA. No plans were required and in the early years none were produced, nor was there "a paperwork nightmare." The procedure for promulgating regulations was simple. State and federal scientists, with industry representatives present and participating, convened once a year and reviewed available data on the status of the shrimp stocks. They prepared recommendations for the three ASMFC commissioners (one each from the administration, legislature, and industry) from each state. [41] The nine commissioners then held a one-day public hearing on the recommendations. Immediately following the hearing, the commissioners then and there decided what regulations to promulgate; the commissioners had regulatory authority entirely unto themselves. There was no anonymous and protracted review and no uncertainties in the process. The industry was generally

---

[41] Note that the commissioners to ASMFC, as mandated by Congress, could be heavily dominated by industry if the legislative commissioner were also a member of the fishing industry. Apparently this possibility did not trouble Congress.

content with the process. It might not like the regulations (the commissioners in 1978 saw fit to close the shrimp fishery for the year), but there was no uncertainty, no months or years of waiting to learn of the rules. The industry and fishermen knew immediately what the regulations would be and could make their plans accordingly. More important, the process gave the commissioners full authority to use their best judgment, to make corrections in management of shrimp from year to year, and, in this experimental business of fisheries management, to make mistakes *and to learn from and correct their mistakes in a timely fashion.* The importance of an opportunity to learn from mistakes is not to be underestimated. NEFMC, because of the extensive review process, does not have that opportunity. There is no evidence that ASMFC management of shrimp ever suffered much from the lack of a plan, with its "paperwork nightmare," or lack of an extensive review process as mandated by MFCMA.

7) The Role of Science

Science not ignored

The role of science looms large in most criticisms of the council's performance. That the council failed to heed - or ignored - the advice of the scientists (or similar comments) is an often-heard accusation and condemnation. Weber (2002:177), for example, states:

> Although the New England debacle revealed a number of weaknesses in the Magnuson-Stevens Act's management system, none were more troubling than the ability of the New England Fishery Management Council to ignore scientific advice and to allow, even defend, overfishing in order to meet short-term economic and social demands.

The charge was repeated by Crockett (2005:194) who asserted that NEFMC is "notorious for ignoring scientific advice... a pattern of delay and denial."

The council, of course, did not ignore scientific advice. The record of council actions makes clear that the council was trying to limit the catch to the levels recommended by the scientists. It is one thing to calculate how many fish should be taken; it is another thing to figure out how to limit the catch to the appropriate level. The question before the council always was *how* to do that in a practical and effective way, and there was little or no specific scientific advice to that end. But the implication of Weber's statement is that all the council had to do was to adopt scientific advice and all would be well.

The position that all the council had to do was adopt the

recommendations of scientists for practical control of fishing, even if there had been any, does not, for several reasons, withstand close scrutiny. It must be said, first, that the scientists were generally correct in a *qualitative* sense in their assessments that told the council that the stocks were not in good shape and were declining in numbers. We cannot recall a time in the first ten years of the council history when council members seriously doubted that advice. They might be skeptical of particular quotas, but not of scientific advice on the general conditions of the stocks. Indeed, the National Research Council (1999:19) made the same basic point: "Although assessments and statistics from... NMFS provide only an imperfect characterization of the status of... U.S. fisheries, the assessments - corroborated by many kinds of evidence - appear to provide a reasonably accurate description of the overall picture." NRC (1999:34) also warned against "an overreliance on the science and culture of quantitative stock assessment (Walters and Maguire 1996)."

The record of NEFMC is clear that it was trying to abide by scientific advice. Of course in 1977 the council had adopted in its entirety and with hardly any hesitation the management plan prepared for it by the scientists of NMFS; within three months the council was faced with serious problems inherent in that plan. In hindsight, or with the benefit of practical management experience, those problems would have been predictable. And it is evident that NMFS was wrong in its judgment in the 1977 plan that its quotas could be adhered to without hardship to the industry. After 1986, the several amendments to the groundfish plan, particularly Amendments 7, 9 and 13, are explicit that the council was trying to abide by scientific advice from its TMG and NMFS's SARC.

Even recognizing the imprecision of stock assessment advice, which we will consider shortly, the major problems were not primarily with the scientific advice. The Task Force (Rothschild et al. 1980:5), commenting on the range of information needed for a management plan, reported to the council that

the best available fishery information is most often limited when compared to the amount generally thought to be required for management. Practical objectives must therefore be consonant with strategic objectives, but they must also not require information beyond that readily available unless plans for acquiring more data and information accompany them.

The additional data to which The Task Force referred is that necessary to develop a plan for the achievement of *public policy* objectives – which lie beyond the realm of traditional fisheries science and which we will review in detail later in this discussion.

Limitations of scientific advice

Before exploring those other non-scientific factors, it is well to note some limitations of scientific advice. It is generally acknowledged that fisheries science is not very precise and is often incomplete. Weber (2002:91) wrote:

> The Magnuson-Stevens Act emphasized basing decisions on the best scientific information available. Often, however, the best scientific information was not very good. Even in the Alaska and New England regions, where the federal government had carried on fisheries research to support international management for decades, critical information often was lacking. Research and information on the socioeconomic dimensions of the fisheries lagged even further behind.

Weber (2002:153) also referred to the "uncertainty and imprecision" of scientific advice. One of the preeminent fisheries scientists, John Gulland, wrote of the limitations of science:

> It is obviously a fallacy to think that scientists, given time, and perhaps also money, can produce the complete answer to management problems; e. g., specify the precise value of the maximum sustained yield from a particular stock of

fish, and also the exact levels of fishing, and of population abundance required to produce it....Scientific finality cannot be achieved. Science advances by disproof rather than proof; a succession of hypotheses are put forward capable of explaining the observed facts, and have to be abandoned or revised as further observations show them to be inadequate. Complete and final scientific advice cannot therefore be provided; all that can, or should, be provided, is advice that is sufficiently accurate and detailed for the immediate purpose (Gulland 1971:473).

The Task Force report (Hennemuth et al. 1980:3,4) considered the problem of scientific uncertainty:

Regulating a fishery to achieve "optimal stock size" is of little use as an objective if optimal stock size can not be established, or indeed, if stock size cannot be measured at all with sufficient precision.

Overfishing and depletion are nebulous terms if their "prevention" is considered outside of the context of optimum yield. A depleted stock is sometimes defined as one which has fallen below the maximum point on yield or stock-recruitment curves. However, the observed variability in productivity of fish stocks is often too large to apply the underlying theoretical models on which such definitions are based. Overfishing, therefore, would better be evaluated in terms of management, that is, social objectives. If it is seen that a population, in the course of pursuing such objectives, is becoming unacceptably low (in the national sense), then the objectives should be revised, since it is probably possible to fish a stock to the point that it will no longer support a continuing fishery.

Even though there was little doubt that the scientific advice on the condition of the stocks was generally correct, it is also true that the numerical estimates of the assessments could be from thirty to fifty percent, or more, in error. (We will note this problem shortly with respect to herring assessments in the Gulf of Maine.) That is to say, the assessment advice was largely qualitative rather than quantitative in nature. And this is a serious problem for managers who are trying to balance all the other issues of management that MFCMA and its concept of OY require them to consider. For example, the *rate* at which a stock should be restored to an appropriate level of biomass may have very significant social and economic consequences for the fishing industry. A fish stock could be restored to a desired level of biomass in five years with certain costs; it could be restored in ten years at presumably much less cost. Or, equally, a ten-year restoration schedule could be of greater cost, depending on what social and economic impacts the managers consider important and how their costs are calculated and balanced. Thus in a hard-pressed industry it is important to get that rate of restoration right. But if the assessment has a thirty-to-fifty percent margin of error, finding the "right" rate is very difficult. We could cite other problems of this kind that arise from the imprecision of the assessments.

Weber (220:202) wrote that the "fishery management councils often interpreted the scientific uncertainty... as a justification for allowing high levels of fishing." It is our recollection, however, that the New England council did not use the imprecision of scientific advice as an excuse or a reason to permit high quotas or overfishing. (The council in fact tried to set its OYs within the confidence limits around the quotas proposed by the scientists.) Rather, the scientific uncertainties significantly increased the difficulties of the council in its attempts to identify effective management measures to achieve the quotas or OYs recommended to it by NMFS; that is, without the benefit of numerical values for the status of stocks with which they could be confident, the council was in the position of having little solid base from which to design a management plan the efficacy of which it could have some degree of confidence.

The dilemma for the council of imprecise assessments was illustrated in a dramatic manner in 2003 by two independent assessments of the status of herring in the Gulf of Maine.

Canadian and United States fisheries scientists, equally respected in their field, produced estimates of stock biomass that differed by a factor of nearly three; one assessment suggested a herring biomass of 600,000 tons, the other of 1.6 million tons - a spread of one million tons. The Canadians and Americans used different methods to produce their estimates, but managers are concerned much more with results than with methods; they need to have a figure in which they can be confident when proposing their regulations. Independent respected scientists from the west coast were asked to try to reconcile the results of these herring assessments or to explain the reasons for the discrepancy. They (Hilborn and Valero 2004:3) concluded "that the current stock size could be not only anywhere between 600,000 tons and 1.6 million tons, but also it could be lower or higher... The data available are not able to provide reliable estimates."

These conclusions reinforce our earlier concern that what is the "best science available", which is required by law as the basis of management, is, in some cases, a matter of opinion, and the "best" may not in fact be very good at all. The managers, then, are left with no useful scientific advice to guide them.

Further, Hilborn and Valero (2004:4) wrote:

> What we do know from the history of fisheries assessments is that *the assessments are often wrong*. Most people are familiar with the Canadian Northern Cod history, where the stock size published in assessments was shown to be more than twice as high as the real stock size. *Similar errors have been found in many if not the majority of fisheries assessments* when they have been evaluated retrospectively (Hilborn 2003). Modern stock assessment methods have become highly complex and difficult to understand (emphasis added).

Hilborn and Valero are not alone in their criticism of fisheries science. George Rose (1997:365-7) wrote:

...the failure of fisheries science and scientific institutions to provide adequate stock information upon which to base management must be acknowledged....The management paradigm for most groundfish involves setting a catch quota based on a target fishing mortality. This follows the modern fisheries paradigm, wherein a quota derived from a population model is thought a sufficient tool to manage stocks. It is a grandiose notion....As a historical experiment, this paradigm can be judged harshly, with a legacy of depleted fisheries.

This judgment was reinforced: "By 1999, it could be said that there was 'growing evidence from fisheries around the world that the current scientific methods and associated data used to provide advice for fish-stock management are failing systematically'" (McGlade 1999, quoted by Pauly and MacLean 2003:24).

The uncertainty goes beyond that of assessment techniques. It lies, also, within the biology of fish stocks themselves. As The Task Force (Hennemuth et al. 1980:6) pointed out, "attempting to influence recruitment by manipulating population size is an uncertain endeavor, since the effect of spawning upon recruitment is itself uncertain." And Guy Marchessault, after his experience for eleven years as the first fisheries scientist with the council, commented on the "demonstrated futility of trying to manage with measures that are predicated upon real-time knowledge of the status of individual stocks and the false belief that these measures can be meaningfully applied to effect stock-specific fishing mortality."

There is also the question of the level of biomass to which stocks should be restored and maintained. The Task Force (Rothschild et al. 1980:5) noted:

> objectives phrased in terms of maintaining a particular stock size, a minimum stock size, or a particular number of spawners, also cause problems. There is often little or no theoretical guidance on the appropriate stock size and if

there were, there would be uncertainty as to when the stock had actually reached the appropriate theoretical level. In any event, manipulating stock size is really a method to achieve some social goal.

That stock size or level of biomass intended "to achieve some social goal" may range from that of a pristine, unexploited stock to that biomass which gives some confidence against the possibility of biological extinction of the stock. These two levels encompass a very wide range indeed. Which one, or some level between the two, is chosen as a management objective is a matter of judgment based upon social, not scientific, considerations. The law, MFCMA, recognizes this fact. It specifies that the objective of management shall be "optimum yield" which is based upon that level that provides "maximum sustainable yield" *as modified by other relevant considerations*. Thus there was no legislatively specified level of biomass to which stocks should be restored. Congress left that to the judgment of the councils.

The false hope of MSY

Critics may object that the level of biomass to be achieved by management should be constrained by the concept of maximum sustainable yield; in fact MFCMA was amended in 1996 toward that end. MSY looms large in the current debates and confrontations about the efficacy of fisheries management, particularly in New England. But the New England council in the summer of 1977, very early in its career, was urged by senior NMFS scientists to abandon the concept of MSY as meaningless. The Task Force (Hennemuth et al. 1980:5) noted:

> Regrettably from the point of view of practical manage-
> ment this model [MSY] does not describe what often
> happens in nature. It assumes that the numbers of young
> added to a population are proportional to the numbers of
> adults, while practical experience with most fish
> populations has shown this to be untrue.... What is wrong,
> then, with the simple model underlying the concept of

maximum sustainable yield? In general, it is deficient in that it treats the population's environment as fixed, whereas in fact natural environments are dynamic, that is to say, in a state of constant flux... The relationships between species may be exceedingly complex... Such relationships may be quite difficult to decipher, and even more difficult to predict.

Weber (2002:13) summarized the development of the concept of MSY, noting that its development and adoption was "the gold standard for modern fisheries management." But he went on to note:

Like other, later scientific formulations that were incorporated in fisheries policy, the limitations of MSY... were largely ignored by decision makers and often by scientists. Among other shortcomings, these models assumed that the environment itself did not fluctuate and that interactions among fish populations had minimal effect. Neither assumption was borne out in reality.

Weber pointed out other shortcomings of the concept of MSY. Further, Weber (2002:100) referred to Lee Talbot, a member of the President's Council on Environmental Quality and a manager of a conservation program at the Smithsonian Institution. Talbot and others, with specific reference to marine mammals, expressed little confidence that the continued use of MSY as a standard would lead to anything but overexploitation. Weber quoted Talbot: "Maximum sustainable yield was an elegant formulation, a generalization of the idealized way that species behave. It was great for training, but was never intended for managing wildlife."

Weber further quoted Carleton Ray:

Science can be just as obstinate and reactionary as any other field. And the traditionalists in science were the population dynamicists, who were very conservation-oriented, but felt that the key was better use of MSY. In fact, when MSY first came around everyone thought it was a breakthrough in conservation, and it turned out to be one of the problems. Now, it's been shown, more or less, that we were right: In management, you can't separate our animals from their environment.

And Lee Alverson (2002:13) concluded that "our preoccupation with setting MSY as a management target, and not just an academic explanation of how stocks might respond to fishing under unlikely assumptions, led to MSY being a part of the problem rather than the 'grand solution.'" Thirty years earlier, shortly before the councils began their work, Peter Larkin (1972:195) similarly observed: "Most important, we [should] stop paying lip service to puritanical notions like maximum sustained yield and come to grips with the more complex problems of real life resource management." And just as NMFS scientists were advising the council to ignore the concept of MSY, Larkin (1977) published "An epitaph for the concept of Maximum Sustained Yield" - "We bury it with the best of wishes/ Especially on behalf of fishes" - in which he (p. 3) quoted John Gulland (1969): "it is very doubtful if the attainment of the maximum sustained yield from any one stock of fish should be the objective of management except in exceptional circumstances." Larkin (1977:3) wrote:

In many ways, it is a pity that now, just when the concept of maximum sustained yield has reached worldwide distribution and is on the verge of worldwide application, it must be abandoned. But that's the way it goes with things we believe.

In fact, an attempt to achieve MSY can be worse than meaningless; it can be destabilizing to particular stocks of fish and to some fisheries systems, as we shall see when we consider the nature of ecosystems. Further, to limit management objectives to MSY rather than OY would seem to foreclose important options, as a number of nations participating in the Law of the Sea Conferences foresaw, and as we shall consider later when we review the purposes or objectives of management.

Scientific predictability

Further, scientific advice in fisheries generally has very little predictive value. [42] This is widely recognized if infrequently mentioned, although The Task Force (Hennemuth et al. 1980:3) did note that fisheries prediction "is only rarely completely achievable in practice." An assessment of the state of the stocks is a measure of the stocks condition when the assessment was made; [43] it is of very little help in predicting the status of stock two or three or more years from now. And because of the often years-long delays caused by the legal requirements and review processes for implementing a fishery management plan under MFCMA, that is the time frame of interest to the council.

There are really two reasons why traditional scientific assessments have very little predictive value. The first reason is the nature of the assessment technique itself. It is essentially a book-keeping procedure whereby the various year-classes represented in the annual investigations at sea and from samplings of the commercial landings of fish are added up and kept track of from year to year. It could be likened to the stock inventory of a hardware store that says very little about next year's sales expectations. The second reason is because the relationship between a stock size and its spawning success is very uncertain (e. g., Sissenwine 1984); in fact there is hardly a case in fisheries science that shows a clear relationship between stock size and future recruitment to the fishery in which one could have

---

[42] A number of scientific papers discuss the low predictability of fisheries, e. g., Gavaris 1993.

[43] Even less frequently mentioned is the fact that assessments become more reliable the further back in time they go. That is, an assessment of a year-class this year is not very precise, but it is pretty good for that same year class five years in the past - which is not really of much help to the manager today who is not much concerned with the status of the stock five years ago.

confidence. "Although the intuitive expectation is that the more spawning adults there are in the population, the more recruits there will be, most fish populations do not show such a relationship" (NRC 1999:34). The Gulf of Maine cod stock is one of the few that seem to show this relationship (NRC 1999:35). Only in the most general terms would one say that a lot of fish will produce a lot of young and that few fish will produce few young. But those are very shaky generalization, and there are known spawning failures from "healthy" stocks, and unexpected successes from very reduced stocks [44]. We look at this question of predictability of future stock sizes in some detail here because it is so important to effective fisheries management.

Fisheries scientists are well aware of the minimal predictive power of Virtual Population Analysis, the book-keeping exercise that is the foundation of stock assessments. Considerable effort is therefore devoted to finding useful predictive indices. It is a common theme of these efforts that the key to prediction will be found at the very earliest life stages of marine organisms; that it is the survival success of larval or post-larval stages that is the critical determinant for the numbers of a particular year-class at the harvestable stage. This view seems to be widely held within fisheries science. The search therefore is for the critical link between an environmental parameter of some kind and the life or death of the larvae. That is to say, perhaps the fate of larvae depends upon an optimal temperature, or perhaps upon finding food at a critical time. The hypothesis is that if the larvae find that food or enjoy an appropriate temperature, then all is well and they will grow, at calculated rates of growth and mortality along the way, without further, or with calculable, uncertainty to the age or size at which they may be harvested.

This hypothesis, it may be noted in passing, is what is known as a *deterministic* approach to prediction. It assumes a one-to-one, cause-and-effect relation between the assumed environmental variable and the fate of larvae; the fate of the larvae is determined

---

[44] Reasons for this are explored in Apollonio 2002.

by the environmental variable. It may also be called a *reductionist* approach to the problem; cause and effect are reducible to a simple, direct relationship. One may note that in spite of considerable efforts to find such a relationship, there has so far been quite modest success. This may simply be a reflection of the difficulty of working within the complexities of the ocean environment. But more likely it is because the world, in the words of Karl Popper (1990), "is causally 'open'." Popper "maintained that the deterministic realm where forces and laws prevail is but a small, almost vanishing, subset of all real phenomena. The latter are suffused with indeterminacies that confound efforts at deterministic prediction" (Ulanowicz 1997:8). Robert Ulanowicz (1997) explored the ecological implications of the 'causally open' nature of systems; we simply note that because of this reality there is a fundamental reason to suspect that the deterministic or reductionist approach to fish prediction is not likely to be useful.

Although we do not attempt to explain Popper's reasoning (Ulanowicz (1997) did that persuasively), in that context we may look with a skeptical eye at a specific example of a deterministic effort to predict fisheries recruitment. In recent years there has been a multi-institutional effort involving a number of scientists to forecast the stock levels of Maine lobsters. The effort continues in 2008. "They hope to discover which factors in the marine environment influence the supply of larval lobsters and affect their ability to successfully settle and survive on the seabed" (Anon. Bigelow Laboratory for Ocean Sciences Annual Report 2000-2002). Note that there are three different issues here: the factors affecting the supply, the successful settlement, and the survival of lobster larvae. Each by itself is a substantial question. Apparently the hypothesis is that there is, for each issue, a cause-and-effect relationship dependent upon a particular environmental factor. But it is hardly likely that it would be the same environmental factor that is important for each of the three issues. And it may well be that the important factor for each issue may differ from year to year. Let us consider why this may be so.

We must first consider the nature of larvae themselves, or in fact the nature of the very young of any species. Simply put, they are fragile and very vulnerable to a wide variety of potential problems. This is equally true of larval lobsters and human infants. The difference between the two is primarily that infants have parents to care for them in the vulnerable years; larval lobsters do not - they are on their own from the moment of egg release. New-born organisms are vulnerable to a variety of dangers, whether it be disease, predation, inadequate nutritional reserves at birth, lethal or sub-lethal temperatures, or inappropriate or insufficient food after birth. Lobster larvae, in addition, are subject to the dangers of finding themselves in ocean currents or circulations or local and temporary eddies that are going the wrong way from the larvae's point of view. The point is that all new-born organisms are vulnerable to many deleterious factors of the environment, any one of which could be fatal at a particular time, and all of which might be fatal at some time or other. This is why Karl Popper says that reality is suffused with indeterminacies. This is why creatures like lobsters and codfish produce so many young. On average, in stable populations, of the tens of thousands or millions produced at each female's spawning, only two will survive the multiple and varying hazards of their environment to make it to their age of reproduction. (If more or less than two, on average, survive, then the population will either increase or decrease.) NMFS acknowledges this reality: "The number of very young fish surviving in the water column varies tremendously from year to year as a result of a large number of physical and biological factors." (Fogarty n.d.:15).

Suppose that we were successful in finding a correlation this year between temperature and the supply of larvae, there is an equally good chance that next year the correlation would not hold; that some other factor could be determinant. And this difficulty applies also to the other two issues of lobster larvae - settlement and survival. The challenge of finding a predictive index at this level thus becomes compounded many fold. One must also recognize and acknowledge the possibility of synergistic effects - either good or bad - at each of the levels, or among them all combined. And this may be the reason the search to date has had limited success. Gislason et al. (2000:469) wrote: "the sometimes heated debate about stock-recruitment relationships... reveals how little we know about the factors responsible for generating either the shape of or the variability around the stock recruitment relationships for even the most intensively studied fish populations."

A prerequisite of predictive capability in general is that there be some limits around the possible dynamics of the phenomenon of interest; that is, if infinitely (or nearly so) variable behavior is possible, then the chances of predicting behavior are negligibly small. Possible behavior must bump against some limits if there is to be predictability. The limits around the possible dynamics of fish eggs or larvae are large, or remote, when the focus of attention is one the larvae themselves. But such limits become much more restrictive within the context of a fisheries system. The nature of ecosystems (O'Neill et al. 1986) is such that a more profitable search for predictive capability should be undertaken not at the very earliest life stages of marine organisms but rather at a higher level wherein lie significant constraints upon dynamics of the whole system and its components, which possibility we will explore further along.

Because of these several problems, it may be that the future of traditional fisheries science as it has been practiced over the last several decades is in doubt. Doubts were expressed by a group of leading fisheries scientists as early as 1981: "existing modeling efforts have reached a point of declining marginal productivity" (Rothschild et al. MS.1982:21-2), and Hilborn (2003:19) wrote:

> The institutional and legal requirements for stock assess-ment, particularly in the U.S., means that our [the scientists's] actual contact with and understanding of fisheries is diminishing rapidly, and we are playing technical games with models that are becoming less relevant to the real fishery.

At least some fisheries scientists will disagree with Hilborn's statement, of course, but one may wonder how many managers, most of whom are not scientists, understand the scientific models upon which their decisions must be based.

Considering the necessarily limited role of science in fisheries management, it may be noted that scientists never, in fact, made a recommendation to NEFMC for *tactics* of management, after the first management plan of 1977, beyond a general admonition to "reduce effort." We might say that that advice was hardly necessary because the council as a whole knew very well - it never doubted - that effort reduction was necessary. That general advice to reduce effort was not very helpful: the real question always was *how* to reduce effort *in a truly effective way*. Perhaps the scientists were reluctant to offer suggestions for specific management measures in deference to the council's responsibility for management (even though NMFS seemed to believe the council's were only advisory in nature). But without doubt the council would have welcomed such practical advice from any source; the history of the council makes clear its efforts to restrain and limit effort. And the council also had to anticipate and try to deal with the often adverse consequences of the various possible tactics for reduction of effort - and these were not inconsequential. We consider the consequences of limited entry, for example, at some length later.

Managers are clearly faced with two substantial problems with respect to scientific advice. First, when it is not wrong, as Hilborn (2003) suggests is often the case, it may be of such imprecision that it can be of little assistance to managers struggling with hard choices in heavily exploited fisheries. Second, it has little to say about what objectives should be chosen for fisheries management or how to attain them.

Non-scientific issues

The main problems of management confronting NEFMC lie not within the realm of science, but rather within the realm of management that is beyond pure science. To illustrate the distinction between science and management we note the comments of Eldon Greenberg, who served as general counsel for NOAA in the early years of MFCMA, as quoted by Weber (2002:93): "I think the New England groundfish fishery was our big failure. I don't think we did a good job of managing New England groundfish then or later, for that matter. I'm not sure they've ever done a good job in managing that fishery. We did not impose the kind of strict management measures, which in retrospect it seems were clearly needed." But like other critics of the New England council, Greenberg apparently did not specify *what* strict management measures he had in mind that should have been imposed. It is true that strict management measures can serve conservation ends, but Hilborn, Punt, and Orensanz (2004:504) wrote:

> The International Pacific Halibut Commission was able to achieve good biological management by intensive regulation, producing a fishing season that often lasted for only 24 hours and was characterized by incredible overcapitalization, economic waste, loss of life, and illegal fishing.

It would be hard to be persuaded that strict measures - "intensive regulation" - with such dismal economic, human, and social consequences are good *management*; good conservation, perhaps, but not good management.

It was those kinds of unintended consequences experienced in the halibut fishery that the New England council tried to avoid as it struggled to develop its plans and regulations. Strictly scientific information and advice must be balanced against other and important considerations.

We cannot recall any specific measures recommended by the federal agencies throughout the first ten years of the council beyond the initial plan of 1977 which very quickly led to very difficult problems. It is true that NMFS strongly recommended the *concepts* of limited entry or ITQs, but advice of such generality in the absence of a specific proposal relevant to the complex, multispecies New England fisheries is not helpful.

Weber (2002:169) asked a key question bearing upon the role of science in fishery management: "Why had fish populations in New England declined so catastrophically when their biology had been so thoroughly studied and analyzed?" Weber did not answer his question, but two things may be implied by the question: 1) that those thorough biological studies and analyses were insufficient for the purpose, and/or 2) that factors other than biological knowledge contributed to the declines. Perhaps Weber meant to imply that with an abundance of biological information the declines could only have been from deficient management. And Weber (2002:153) further noted: "Whatever the setting or decision-making body, however, management decisions did not begin and end with scientific advice and analysis." This author apparently intended by this somewhat ambiguous statement to be critical of managers who did not *confine* their decisions to scientific advice. But it must be recognized that biological or fisheries science, as such, is only one element of the process of fisheries management. Management is a matter of setting and implementing public policy, and as such management must also be concerned with economics, equity among participants, social matters, and similar non-biological or non-scientific issues. Formally stated management objectives themselves reflect this reality. The various fisheries management plans prepared in the first ten years of the council's [plural] histories included a number of issues or objectives that were not directly related to scientific matters in the usual sense of the word. The National Standards of the MFCMA stated that Optimum Yield, the mandated overall purpose of all plans, [45] shall take into account other relevant non-

---

[45] A purpose of MFCMA was "...4) to provide for the preparation and implementation, in accordance with national standards, of fishery management plans which will achieve and maintain, on a continuing basis, the optimum yield from each fishery." Sec.2 (b)(4).

scientific factors. [46]

Finally, considering non-scientific issues in fisheries management, issues upon which "science" can have no special advice, consider once again the question of the proper level of biomass to which stocks should be restored, or the rate at which they should be restored to that level. Or which segment of the diverse fishing industry should be allowed to catch what percentage of the allowable catch. These are not scientific issues. They are public policy issues - and usually highly contentious. Science here can offer no advice that is more relevant than advice from any other interested entity. It is the council's responsibility with the information available to it, and within its own experience and judgment, to make those decisions. Peter Larkin (1980:251) referred to U.S. and Canadian efforts "to embrace all the considerations that might guide fisheries management... It is a major implication of their approaches that there is no single way of managing fisheries, and regional 'councils' must have a large say in making decisions."

---

[46] MFCMA stated: "The term 'optimum', with respect to the yield from a fishery, means the amount of fish - A) which will provide the greatest overall benefit to the Nation, with particular reference to food production and recreational opportunities; and B) which is prescribed as such on the basis of the maximum sustainable yield from such fishery, as modified by any relevant economic, social, or ecological factor." Sec. 3 (18).

8) Defining Objectives

John Gulland (1974:105) wrote: "Everybody concerned with fishing will have slightly different ideas on what the proper objective of fishery management should be." Gulland's observation is not a negligible or trivial reality; it can be a contentious issue in fisheries management. We noted earlier that the Stratton Commission of the 1960s identified the primary purpose of management as the development of the U.S. fishing industry. That purpose also was a large part of the intent of Congress when it enacted MFCMA in 1976. With time, the purpose has changed dramatically; it is now to restrain the development of the fishing industry.

Initial absence of objectives

The original New England groundfish plan of 1977 as published in the Federal Register [47] contained twenty-six pages of rather irrelevant "geophysical" and socio-economic descriptions of and tables for the waters and regions under council jurisdiction, but there were no stated objectives for the plan. It did contain the statement: "Purpose: Regulations of this Section shall apply to domestic fishermen that take haddock (*Melanogrammus aeglefinus*, cod (*Gadus callarias*) and yellowtail flounder (*Limanda ferruginea*) beginning March 1, 1977, in that portion of the Atlantic Ocean in which the United States exercises exclusive fishery management authority." The closest it came to a clear objective was the statement "United States management... will be formulated to attain Optimum Yield from the various species" with an expectation that Optimum Yield of stocks would be

---

[47] March 14, 1977 Pt. III.

attained in three to seven years. The plan did not define OY (recall that MFCMA itself defined it as that which provides the greatest overall benefits to the nation) as it might bear upon cod, haddock, and yellowtail flounder. The plan concluded with the unsupported statement that "thus, the measures proposed are totally beneficial in effect," but it did not explain in what way the plan would be beneficial. These characteristics, or what in hindsight are substantial deficiencies, of the plan passed without comment at that time by the council or by the public, but they would lead to trouble. For example, early in 1978 NOAA warned the council that NOAA would not "accept overfishing." MFCMA did not define overfishing, nor did NOAA, nor did the NMFS plan, and because the term can only be defined with reference to OY or other stated objectives, which were not defined in the 1977 groundfish plan, the NOAA warning was simply blustering and meaningless.

An advisory report (Anon. MS 1977:passim) prepared in 1977 at the request of the council pointed out that "Objectives must achieve the seven National Standards" contained within the MFCMA, but that "the National Standards are pretty vague....the National Standards themselves must be interpreted before objectives are chosen to achieve them. At least the following terms must be defined: Optimum Yield, Overfishing, Efficiency, and Capacity." The report noted that a definition of OY requires consideration of relevant ecological, economic, and social factors. The report, for discussion purposes and by way of examples, noted and analyzed three possible and legitimate management objectives for hakes, six possible objectives for scallops and one for herrings. It noted (Anon. MS 1977:34) that

> the council must recognize that no matter how elegant the data, [its choice of objectives] will require judgment and often *highly experimental* management measures....The need to make many experimental decisions without adequate information reinforces the council mission to develop FMPs that meet national standards in a step-by-step management approach....The information requirement of comprehensive

fisheries management in the Fishery Conservation Zone (FCZ) are *enormous*....Much of this necessary information (biological as well as economic/social) has yet to be developed. The council [should] establish... procedures in the near term that are as simple as possible pending additional information (emphasis added).

The report concluded that "the complexity of the law [MFCMA] nearly *invites* [legal] battles....complex approaches offer more subjects for disputes and legal intervention," a notable forecast of things to come. The complexity of the law, of course, has increased considerably since 1977.

Undefined Optimum Yield

NOAA and NMFS very early recognized the vague nature of OY as the objective of MFCMA and that it could cause problems as a goal for fisheries management. The agencies organized a national conference in the spring of 1977 to clarify the issue. As the chairman of the New England council reported to the council, [48] "the Optimum Yield Conference made clear that the criteria for determining Optimum Yield must vary between councils and between fisheries." But this apparent consensus was later disputed by a member of the council (who later became the NMFS Regional Administrator) who maintained that "the intent of Optimum Yield was to remove an element of judgment in management and substitute quantified factors in management decisions." [49] This opinion reflected the view of the Acting Administrator of NOAA (who as a Senate staff member had participated in drafting MFCMA) who wrote: [50] "...under the law the optimum yield of any fishery is the legal upper limit of harvest for that fishery and not merely a 'target.'" In fact, it may

---

[48] council minutes, July 5-6, 1977

[49] council minutes, July 5-6, 1977

[50] Letter from James P. Walsh to Edward J. MacLeod, June 28, 1978.

reasonably be argued that MFCMA did not set OY as the legal upper limit for a catch. A review of MFCMA from a legal perspective (Bean 1983:393; Bean and Rowland 1997:158) noted that

> The use of concepts like "greatest overall benefit" and "relevant" social factors obviously vests the Councils and the Secretary with a great deal of discretion in making this crucial determination [i. e., optimum yield]. The only element of the determination that is more or less capable of precise quantification is that of "maximum sustainable yield." That element, however, is clearly intended to serve only as the point of departure for a determination of optimum yield. How the Councils or the Secretary choose to depart from that standard is probably beyond any effective judicial review.

These authors, citing the Code of Federal Regulations, wrote:

> Quotas may exceed optimum yield in any given year. The specification of [optimum yield] in an FMP... is not automatically a quota or ceiling, although quotas may be derived from the [optimum yield] where appropriate (50 CFR 602.11(g)(1) 1995). [And further]: Exceeding [optimum yield] does not necessarily constitute overfishing, although they might coincide. Even if no overfishing resulted, continual harvest at a level above a fixed value [optimum yield] would violate national standard 1 because [optimum yield] was exceeded (not achieved) on a continuing basis (50 CFR 602.11(g)(2) 1995) (Bean and Rowland 1997:158-9, fn64).

In major amendments to MFCMA in 1996, the definition of OY

was modified so that it could not exceed MSY. [51] The intent of proponents of the modified definition was to insert scientific objectivity and certitude into council decisions, to reduce or eliminate arbitrary judgments resulting from the vague nature of OY as defined in 1976, and to insure that catches would not exceed MSY and that stocks would not be "overfished." Weber (2002:202) noted that "Reformers were intent on ending the use of uncertainty in estimating sustainable fishing levels to meet short-term demands for increasing or maintaining fishing levels." But it is clear that simply restricting the definition of OY so that it could not exceed MSY is to lean on a "weak reed," indeed, so long as the concept of MSY itself is a very questionable scientific proposition. We have noted that on at least two occasions senior scientists with NMFS advised the council of the serious shortcomings of MSY, even to the point in the summer of 1977 of advising the council to abandon the concept for management purposes. Whereas the amendments of 1996 included definitions of OY and overfishing and thus attempted to remove the uncertainties implicit in those terms, they did not attempt the same task for MSY which underlies the MFCMA concepts of OY and overfishing.

The difficulty of defining objectives

The Task Force (Rothschild et al. 1980:3) noted that "identifying fishery management objectives is a critical task. Objectives must

---

[51] The Sustainable Fisheries Act (SFA) of 1996 states: "The term 'optimum', with respect to the yield from a fishery, means the amount of fish which - (A) will provide the greatest overall benefit to the Nation, particularly with respect to food production and recreational opportunities, and taking into account the protection of marine ecosystems; (B) is prescribed as such on the basis of the maximum sustainable yield from the fishery as reduced by any relevant economic, social, or ecological factor: and (C) in the case of an overfished fishery, provides for rebuilding to a level consistent with producing the maximum sustainable yield in such fishery. 104-297(28)."

be realistic and achievable." In view of this statement, we find it
ironic that the purposes of The Task Force itself were not clear,
even to its originators and members. Some understood that it was
to serve as an advisory group, to be called upon occasionally for
technical assistance. But a senior official in NMFS stated that its
purpose was "to develop a comprehensive management plan for
New England mixed fishery including cod, haddock, and yellowtail flounder." [52] His statement was accompanied by a draft
proposal "that a comprehensive plan for the management of New
England groundfish could be expedited through the use of an
expert task force... to propose a series of management alternatives
for decision makers with the short and long range consequences
of each... clearly identified." An information memorandum from
the chief of NMFS, to his boss, the Administrator of NOAA,
stated that the New England council "has agreed with us in a task
group to prepare such an FMP probably for later implementation." [53], [54] Apparently the Assistant Administrator for NMFS
accepted both purposes, advisory and plan preparation, which
probably did little to clarify the question of its purpose for those
who participated on and with The Task Force. The Task Force
report (Hennemuth et al. 1980:1) reflected this uncertainty by
stating a third purpose: "The Northeast Fisheries Management
Task Force was organized in 1979 to provide a forum for
discussion of the major issues which management, government,
and industry must resolve." And its initial report stated yet
another purpose: "Its job will be to address the range of
alternatives available, to assess benefits to be expected from each,
to translate these alternatives into *specific objectives*, and to show,
by way of example, how the alternatives might apply to particular
fisheries" (Hennemuth et al. 1980:1) (emphasis added).

---

[52] Letter from William G. Gordon, Director, Office of Resource
Conservation and Management, March 9, 1979, to the chairman of the
New England council.

[53] From Terry L. Leitzell to Richard A. Frank, March 23, 1979.

[54] Memo to NEFMC and NMFS officials by Paul Draheim, Deputy
Executive Director, NEFMC, April 1979.

But The Task Force with its considerable expertise in fisheries was unable to accomplish objectives that were realistic and achievable. We make this point not to be critical of The Task Force but to make clear and underline the difficulties confronting the council itself. As Dykstra reported to the council at the time, referring to the problems both The Task Force and the council had encountered in defining objectives, "we [council members and Task Force members] began to understand each other."

Clearly understood and articulated objectives are important to fishery management for two reasons. First, objectives have a major bearing on the *kinds* of regulations to be implemented. And second, only by comparison of results with the stated objectives can it be determined whether a plan or regulations are having the intended effect. But it is a fact that no management objectives were explicitly stated for New England groundfish prior to July 1978.

It is true that management plans produced by the several councils in the early years had stated objectives, but they were almost invariably of a rather vague, non-specific character. Such objectives as "restore the fishery to a healthy sustainable condition", typical of many of the objectives in the plans, are little more than platitudes. [55] Such stated objectives gave little or no direction for the management strategies or tactics. And they gave no benchmark for a measurement of success or failure. There is, incidentally, a school of thought that advocates vague objectives because, it believes, vagueness is the only way to obtain consensus on a controversial plan; vagueness lets the purpose

---

[55] One of the authors chaired a public hearing in southern New England on the butterfish plan prepared by the Mid-Atlantic Council. A stated objective of the plan was to minimize the cost of fish to the consumer. The chairman's recitation of this objective, by way of introduction to the plan and the hearing, provoked a memorable outburst from a local fisherman: "Hell, I'm not busting my ass out there to minimize the cost to the consumer!"

reside in the mind of the beholder, and, therefore, rather than arguing about specific objectives which might benefit one party and injure another (a very likely probability of any specific fisheries plan), each party can believe it gets something from the deal - perhaps as much as it can hope to get.

A platitudinous objective leaves unanswered the questions of to what level of numbers or biomass should a stock be restored, or at what rate. And platitudinous objectives do not address the question of the *cost* of achieving the objectives. These specific questions very much affect the operational details of any management plan. There may be implicit in them an assumption that the stocks should be restored to the levels of the "good old days" when fishing was good - say, the 1950s or early 1960s before foreign fishing vessels arrived on Georges Bank and when American fishing vessels pretty much had the traditional fishing grounds to themselves. But that easy assumption may overlook the fact the fishing vessels of the 1970s or 1980s were much more efficient than those of the earlier years. Synthetic net materials, increased understanding of the fishing characteristics and fishing power of mesh configurations and net designs, and the vastly increased capabilities for fish-finding from the advent of remarkable electronics all significantly increased the fishing capacity of fishing vessels. Thus an unspoken or perhaps unrecognized assumption of stock levels of the "good old days" might be inappropriate for the later years; that is, it might require a much larger stock size to sustain the increased fishing power of a larger number of much more efficient fishing vessels.

A further difficulty for identifying and agreeing upon objectives lies in the diversity of the New England fishery. Margaret Dewar (1983) noted that "the inshore and offshore fisheries of New England catch finfish and shellfish: no other generalizations are possible." Among commercial fishermen some species are of particular interest; that is, those species provide the principal livelihood for certain fishermen or certain ports. But for other fishermen, those species are a side issue; they might be a helpful bycatch, providing a supplemental income, but strenuous conservation efforts on their behalf could well impede the efforts of fishermen who are primarily interested in other species. It is true that the various ports of New England focused on different species. Boston at that time favored haddock, New Bedford specialized in scallops and yellowtails, Point Judith landed yellowtails, scup, and butterfish (when available), Gloucester landed herring, whiting, and redfish, Portland landed herring, whiting, and hakes. Of course the landings of the various ports were not limited to these species, but there was certainly a preponderance of interest in and specialized landings of different species among the various ports. Peter Doeringer and his colleagues wrote:

> Although all New England fishing ports have some elements of production, marketing, and labor relations in common, each port has its own identity as an economic system within the fishing industry. Ports specialize in particular species and their fleets fish in different grounds. There are variations in size of vessel and type of gear among New England's fishing ports. There are also differences among ports in the age, education, and ethnicity of the fishing industry's labor force and in its attachment to the industry. Similarly, the ways of adjusting to economic change, the causes of inflexibility in resources committed to the industry, and the consequences of change for jobs and income in the industry are not uniform throughout the New England region (Doeringer, Moss, and Terkla 1986:33).

It should be clear that the ports would have greater or lesser interests in the various species. And so it is evident that a port could be disinclined to support stringent measures for a particular species in which it had only marginal interest if those measures might restrict its catch of its favored species. This situation in fact developed when the scallop fishery on Georges Bank, of major concern to New Bedford, was closed down in order to restore haddock, of minor interest to New Bedford.

Recreational fishermen, a not negligible part of the economy of the fisheries of the region, might have a very different objective in mind from that of commercial fishermen. Such a conflict arose with respect to whiting off southern New England or off the mid-Atlantic states. Recreational fishermen were primarily interested in the opportunity to catch a fish (and possibly release it). They wanted the experience - the likelihood - of getting a bite. An abundance of fish, increasing the probability of getting that bite, therefore was important to them. But commercial fishermen would prefer to catch whiting in such numbers that could result in a level of biomass, even at biologically "sustainable" levels, that would greatly reduce the frequency of recreational fishermen getting a bite. The two objectives are hardly compatible. It is also relevant that for a good many years now, in 2008, there is a continuing struggle between recreational and commercial fishermen for striped bass - whether the species should be managed for recreational or commercial purposes. It is unlikely this debate will ever be resolved, and it greatly complicates the management process.

The problem of defining agreed-upon objectives was not confined to the New England council. In describing the functions of international fisheries commissions, Weber (2002:61) wrote:

> As fishing fleets grew, the effectiveness of... treaty organizations was challenged by several persistent problems: the difficulty of achieving agreement on meaningful conservations measures among nations with different views, *conflicting goals of development and conservation*, risk-prone decision making, fishing by nonmembers, resistance to effective enforcement, the failure to support or act upon scientific analysis, inadequate funding, and the lack of effective monitoring programs (emphasis added).

Defining "simple" objectives

Two or three years into the New England council operations, in the late 1970s and early 1980s, it was clear that the council was dealing with an ever-more confusing and unproductive situation. Its regulations had become numerous and complex, sometimes contradictory, difficult to enforce, and of marginally discernible benefit to the fish stocks. Much of the council's time was then spent on trying to correct the unintended consequences that had been created by its earlier regulations - among them, for example, the regulations that induced split trips and misreported landings, or the rush to get one's share, even at the considerable risk of fishing in bad weather, before a quota was taken and a fishery closed. The feeling began to grow within the council that it was time to back off, to give itself "breathing room", to get out of the relentless press of crisis management, and to try to identify its valid, legitimate, attainable purposes that would have discernible benefits for the fish stocks. It took much time and persuasion to achieve a majority vote within the council to this end. Some council members were never persuaded and some believed that the council had to continue to try to correct the problems of the existing plan. But a majority vote for a new approach was achieved in time. While the fundamental reconsideration was underway, the council implemented what was called the Interim Plan. It was intended to be just that - to provide beneficial if minimal regulations in the interim while a better plan was being developed - even though critics called it a council cop-out. [56] The Interim Plan was intended to replace a complex set of regulations and implement instead a set of simple, relatively uncontroversial, clearly beneficial regulations - minimum fish sizes, minimum mesh sizes, and closures of areas with spawning fish. With those in place, the council hoped that it could escape the time-consuming, soul-destroying, crisis-management meetings that had nearly overwhelmed it. It hoped that it could then focus instead on what it was really trying to do, that is, to effectively control fishing mortality - and how to do it.

The council thought that the fishing industry would find reason to comply with its Interim Plan; a sub-objective of the IP was to

---

[56] Some critics named it for one of its principal council sponsors, not with complimentary intent.

encourage greater compliance with the regulations. It recognized the problems of enforcement and compliance as they affected the success of any management plan, and it drafted a "Statement of Council Policy with Respect to Enforcement of Management Measures or Regulations" wherein it noted that "management measures which are simple, understandable, and consistent with traditional fishing practices may not require a high degree of governmental enforcement to ensure compliance by the industry." Further, "the management experience of the last three years provides ample evidence that a management system which requires a high degree of enforcement to assure compliance will probably not be effective" (Pierce MS 1982:77).

But, wrote Halliday and Pinhorn (1997:103):

> From the beginning of council activities in 1977, the fishing industry showed little acceptance of the need for direct control of fishing mortality, be it through catch limitations or otherwise. This resulted in the adoption of the principle of minimum interference embodied in plans from 1982. The council anticipated that because the fishers appeared to want this approach, they would be willing to comply with those few regulations in the plan. The council also expected that enforcement agencies had the ability to enforce these rules. These expectations were not met. One study showed that in the Georges Bank fishery, regulations were frequently violated by a quarter to a half of all fishers. These violators used illegal mesh on almost all trips and fished in closed areas on about one third of their trips. The council's Technical Monitoring Group pointed out that there were few incentives for fishers to comply with regulations. There were inadequate resources for enforcement, and the plan contained regulations that were difficult to enforce and provided ready loopholes for evasion, so the risk of detection was low.

In this context it is relevant to note the opinion of Hilborn, Punt and Orensanz (2004:493) that "Although existing fisheries management systems are widely recognized to have largely failed... the public and almost the entire scientific community believe that this failure is due to overfishing." (And Alverson (2002:10) listed *nineteen* possible causes of overfishing, with the comment that his list was far from complete.) Hilborn and his colleagues went on to "argue that overfishing is a symptom of poor governance systems rather than the structural disease to be treated....We conclude [that] sustainable fishing will occur when the institutional framework encourages the participants to behave in a way that is societally desirable."

The council's Interim Plan as originally conceived was intended to provide some protection to the stocks and through its intended simplicity to improve the reliability of catch data that had been distorted by efforts to circumvent quotas, to minimize incentives for noncompliance, to avoid controversies within the council, and to allow the council to devote its focused attention toward the development of a new and effective groundfish plan.

But the intended simplicity itself of the Interim Plan created a substantial impediment to its adoption. A number of council members felt that it was too simple, that it contained no "braking mechanism" or "fail-safe" provision. The concern was that a simple plan with no direct controls on fishing effort would lead to greatly increased landings and thus decreased stock numbers; that without some clear and automatic provision to stop excessive fishing, the plan would inevitably lead to further stock declines - to overfishing however defined. There was also concern within the industry that the plan, without limits on fish landings, would lead to catching too many fish, to gluts of fish in the market, and to depressed prices. These concerns, of course, implied unspoken objectives of the plan that were deliberately not intended by the proponents of the plan. Even in its simplest form, the objectives of the plan were either not clear or not acceptable to members of the council. This confusion of purpose became a major impediment to implementation of the plan; instead of being so simple that it could be developed and implemented in a few weeks or months, these implied objectives contributed to the fact that it took more than two and a half years to implement the Interim Plan.

The council debate on the prospect of overfishing under the Interim Plan, and what to do about it, is instructive in the context of defining objectives. Part of the debate took place on October 20 and 21, 1981, (two years after the council had decided to develop the Interim Plan!). The discussion continued on February 25, 1982 and later. In short, the extended discussion was inconclusive in identifying a situation that was to be addressed by a "fail-safe" mechanism to prevent "overfishing" - however defined - or what that mechanism would be.

The council minutes of October and December 1981 and February, June, and July 1982, particularly, are informative on this issue. Here are some verbatim comments from the minutes [57] of the council discussions:

Mr. Guimond: I don't feel that we have to guarantee the economic viability of a business. If that is what our objective is, then we are not talking fish, we are talking the fishery. I don't see anything wrong with allowing the industry to go out and take a risk like any other businessman does, I don't think it is our role to make sure they are economically viable.

Mr. Peterson:... The Act is to promote a viable and healthy industry. I think there is a responsibility on us as managers to make sure the U.S. has a healthy and viable industry in the fishing area.

Mr. Fulham:... I can see very clearly that the conservation of a natural resource, which is owned by everyone, should be our priority concern. The health of someone exploiting that industry should be a concern, but I don't think it should be a priority and equal concern to the preservation of the resource that everyone

---

[57] council minutes, October 20, 1981

owns. [58]

In fact, the council could not define overfishing in this context - as the Development Sciences report in 1977, which we noted before, had warned. Because the council did not or could not define overfishing, it could not identify a point at which a "fail-safe" mechanism would become operative. Finally the council could not decide what that "fail-safe" mechanism might be. Neither "dithering" nor alleged conflict of interest are the reasons why these issues were not resolved. Nor was the council alone in its difficulties of defining these issues. The chairman of The Task Force, established to provide expert advice on these difficult issues, acknowledged: "In terms of communicating effectively what it was we were talking about, we were never quite sure ourselves." [59]

The council groundfish committee met regularly for over a year on this problem. The meetings were serious, time consuming, thoughtful, and unproductive. The committee was never able to develop clearly articulated objectives with sufficient specificity to give the desired sense of direction to the council management policy. The failure was not for lack of trying.

We noted earlier that there were considerable differences of opinion within NEFMC, NOAA, and NMFS as to the purpose of The Task Force. In spite of this uncertainty of purpose, The Task Force functioned for about two years. It "produced a considerable body of technical material and had promoted beneficial dialogue among council members and staff, government representatives, and industry" (quoted in Pierce MS 1982:123). It produced

---

[58] The comments of Mr. Guimond and Mr. Fulham are of interest, incidentally, in the context of the allegations of conflict of interest among council members. Alan Guimond was closely associated with commercial fishing interests and Thomas Fulham owned fishing trawlers out of Boston.

[59] council minutes, June 16, 1982

twenty-six papers, mostly of a factual or technical nature, for example, "Three-Tier Versus Current Fisheries Statistics System" and "Proposed Work Plan for Evaluating Alternative Forms of Management." But even with its undoubted expertise and experience in fisheries and fisheries science and the *theory* of management, The Task Force report noted that it had "not achieved its full potential to serve as a medium for dialogue on problems common to the New England and Mid-Atlantic Management Councils... [and to] deliberate issues that would be too complex to consider in the limited time within which Council meetings take place" (quoted in Pierce MS 1982:123). (There is no mention here of the preparation of a management plan, apparently an original objective of The Task Force.)

The chairman of The Task Force noted that The Task Force "needed the council's guidance in defining the problems that they see as critical issues for Task Force deliberation." In other words, the issue had come full circle; The Task Force had been created in 1979 to provide, in effect, direction to the council and steer it out of its dilemma - that is, the burden of problems to which, the council confessed, it saw no solutions. By March 1982 the Task Force turned to the council for policy guidance, that is, to state its objectives. Without such stated objectives The Task Force found that it could not fulfill its stated purpose, and that, in spite of its broad expertise and considerable experience, it was in no better position than the council itself to identify such objectives. Clearly, if the council had been able to give that guidance, The Task Force would have been unnecessary. The identification of objectives, it became apparent, is a matter of policy, not of science.

Comments, from the council minutes of June 16, 1982, are revealing:

Mr. Hennemuth [then the chairman of The Task Force and the Deputy Director of the NMFS Northeast Fisheries Science Center]:

We are really dealing primarily with what I like to say is the technicalization of politics in management....We had to conclude that we couldn't define in a useful way the management alternatives. Even when we tried to define the simplest aspects, we concluded that we could not assess the impacts; certainly not the social and economic structure of the fisheries. It was a significant finding....I think the council members have to decide what they think are the primary issues....The Task Force wasn't meant to solve anyone's specific problems, but to try to lay out what the very practical problems were. They do deserve to be defined, and we need to indicate where the *unanswerable* questions are (emphasis added).

This was a disappointing conclusion considering that the identification of management alternatives was originally stated to be a principle objective of The Task Force. It is interesting that The Task Force of experts implicitly acknowledged that there were "unanswerable questions." But that gave the council little comfort.

And from the same (June 16, 1982) minutes, council member Dykstra reported to the council:

A lot of [Task Force] people thought they could come up with hard numbers. It turned out that their whole operation was not nearly as perfect as was imagined. They had to make assumptions; and we [council members and task force members] gradually began to understand each other....Several times [the chairmen] attempted to explain what we were doing, and that only made it worse....most of the decisions are *social or political* decisions. Unless you get rid of the mixed trawl fisheries, there are tradeoffs and costs that will be judgment calls....there are some people who think it's simple, but it is a serious problem (emphasis added).

Earlier, Dykstra had reported to the council that one very

beneficial effect of the endeavor was actual education of the Task Force itself. Shortly after 1982 The Task Force faded away. Nothing more was heard of it or its reports.

Here we may recall an observation by Shelley et al. (1996, 234):

> Indeed, a persistent complaint from some New England Council members was that they lacked clear, long-term strategic objectives and that intelligent management was impossible in the absence of such objectives. While that observation may be so, no one on the New England Council took steps to develop such objectives, casting doubt on the motivation of these comments.

Contrary to this assertion, clearly the council and The Task Force made great efforts to identify objectives for the groundfish management plan.

The diversity of possible objectives

There is in fact a wide range of possible and legitimate objectives of fisheries management, all with different consequences for appropriate management strategies and tactics. This is a point that may not be readily apparent. The Stratton Commission (Commission on Marine Science, Engineering and Resources 1969:108) listed a variety of possible management objectives:

- To maximize its net income from the fisheries
- To prevent serious unemployment in fishing communities with no viable alternatives
- To provide fish at the lowest possible price to consumers
- To improve... balance of payments
- To pursue two or more of these aims in varying degrees.

The variety of choices complicates the task of management for several reasons. The first, of course, is the simple recognition that such a range of possible objectives exists. There is then the problem of reaching agreement among managers as to which is their choice. And then there is the task of selecting the management tactics that are appropriate for that choice. And then there is the question whether the perceived benefits of management for that objective are commensurate with the costs.

Some years ago Apollonio was taken to task by the author of a book for general readers on fisheries problems (he can't remember the title or author; he does remember the dressing down). That author castigated Apollonio for his suggestion that "pulse fishing" in some circumstances *may* be a legitimate management policy. She wrote at the time when the foreign fishing fleets off New England, some of whom clearly engaged in pulse fishing, were the villains of the fisheries declines. Pulse fishing is the practice of taking as many fish as rapidly and efficiently as possible without the intent of trying to maintain a stock in such a condition that it could supply a certain biomass of harvestable fish over a sustained period of time - a conventional goal. Pulse fishing is usually practiced in such a way as to minimize costs and thus maximize profits. It often has the purpose of generating large profits from fishing that can then be re-invested in other economic activities that may have a long-term benefit for the country engaged in the practice. Such accumulation of capital may be a very legitimate management objective for that fishery. The National Research Council (1999:13) noted:

> The industrialization occurring in many parts of the world increases the need for foreign currency, and one way to get that currency is to sell seafood. Net fisheries exports in developing countries were worth $U.S. 16 billion in 1994 (FAO 1997a), more than the exports of coffee, bananas, rice and many other commodities (FAO 1997b).

Pulse fishing may in fact reduce a stock of fish to a low level of biomass, but it is hardly likely to eliminate the stock because long before that point would be reached fishing would become expensive and uneconomical and thus negate the objective of pulse fishing - an accumulation of capital. And, further, pulse fishing need not necessarily be injurious in any serious or prolonged way to the stock of fish. Depending upon the particular species, the stock may recover quite rapidly from declines brought on by pulse fishing. Some species, in fact, naturally undergo large variations in numbers and stock sizes. Their fundamental biological characteristics are such that they are well able to recover rather quickly from heavy fishing or other perturbations. Mackerel - a main target of pulse fishing by foreign fleets off New England in the 1970s - is an example. Mackerel did recover rather quickly when pulse fishing ceased. Pulse fishing, then, could be a legitimate management objective for an appropriate species. But other species do not have that capability of rapid recovery and they would suffer greatly from pulse fishing. Pulse fishing would be a completely inappropriate objective or tactic for such species.

All this is to suggest that the objective of management is not so easy to choose, but that the appropriate strategies and tactics of management ought to be determined by whatever objective is chosen. And if the objective is vague or ill-chosen, then the managers are seriously handicapped in deciding what to do by way of management tactics, and they have little help in determining whether their efforts have any benefits.

Social objectives of management

The Task Force (Hennemuth et al. 1980:1) stated that "At bottom management is addressed to social and economic goals which may or may not be served by such traditional approaches as maintaining yields of various species over many years." The Task Force (1980;6) reiterated that position several times: "Fish stocks are managed not for their own sake but to achieve social objectives, and this takes place in a social context....the success of management is to be measured, finally, in social terms." Further, (1980;7): "The social basis of management is implicit in the concept of 'optimum yield'. When judging what that optimum might be, biological and technical facts-of-life must be given full weight, but managers must always have before them the principle that management is intended to serve social ends." And further (1980;8): "Fishery management is intended to increase social benefits from the resource. Thus, choice of management techniques requires *clear* statements of social objectives" (emphasis added). Further: "*How these objectives are defined is crucial to the management process.* To be useful, objectives must be clearly stated, practically attainable, of *measurable* benefit, and based upon an understanding of all aspects of the problem they address, rather than fragments of the problem" (1980:3) (emphasis added). Further: "A clear statement of social objectives must precede formulation of a management strategy, but this is difficult because the perception of what is beneficial may vary from fishery to fishery, and from one social group or region to another." The National Research Council (1999:94) reinforced this reality: "Fishery management is primarily a social process."

Critics of the council may argue that the point of management is to maintain stocks at some particular level of biomass such as that of MSY - indeed, that seems to be the focus of most criticisms of the council and a primary purpose of amendments to MFCMA. The Task Force (Hennemuth et al. 1980:4) stated:

Maintaining a resource in some particular state may be set forth as a management objective, but this often begs the question of why such a state is desirable. There are certain biological constraints on objectives. However, the purposes of management are social, and objectives of management, assuming they are realistic in ecological terms, should be established with reference to the social consequences they are intended to produce.

And Peter Larkin (1980:260) noted that "The fisheries manager cannot responsibly indulge in single mindedness [e. g., focused on achieving MSY]: he must aim for the mistier objectives of social optimization."

We shall find later, also, that if we are in fact to practice ecosystems-based management of fisheries (this idea is sometimes incorrectly characterized as "multispecies management"), as is widely advocated as the only viable alternative to the traditional practice of single-species management, then a clear definition or statement of the objectives of management becomes essential. We shall find that ecosystems cannot be defined in an operational sense - the ecosystem cannot be a useful concept for management - if the objectives of management are vague or non-existent. The fact of the matter is that the operational parameters of a concept of an ecosystem are a function of the agreed-upon objectives, and will change if the objectives are changed. This idea may take some getting used to. For that reason we will return to it later in our discussion of the nature of fisheries ecosystem management.

Defining objectives, then, is an essential but neither an obvious nor easy task for successful fishery management.

Biological reference points

In recent years the attainment of biological reference points (BRPs), a concept that was not conspicuous or prevalent during our terms with the council, 1977-86, has emerged as the objective for groundfish management in New England. "The biological targets are the foundation of the groundfish plan, the base upon which all management measures are built. When a plan doesn't 'achieve' its target, more restrictions are applied" (CFN January 2004:8A). A reference point, as we noted earlier, refers to a particular parameter of a population, such as spawning stock biomass, fishing mortality rates, or re-building rates, expressed numerically. Reference points have the apparent virtue of objectivity and exactitude. Hilborn (2003:16-17) characterized reference points as follows:

> If any "standard" practice in linking stock assessment to decision making has evolved, it is taking the best estimated stock size from an assessment and calculating a recommended harvest by multiplying this stock size by a desired exploitation rate that may change in relation to the stock size... In both the U.S. and Canada a paradigm has

evolved of reference points based on current size in relation to hypothetical unexploited stock size....For each species a target exploitation rate (Uref) and a virgin biomass are defined, and then the recommended TAC is taken by multiplying the best estimated stock size by the target exploitation rate. When uncertainty in current stock size is explicitly considered, one can calculate the best recommended TAC by weighting the probabilities the assessment assigns to different stock sizes. Reference points may be calculated for exploitation rates, or stock biomass. It is becoming increasingly common to use or at least consider precautionary reference points, whose general characteristic is that they aim for larger stock biomass and lower exploitation rates than reference points based on traditional maximum yield objectives.

But Hilborn went on to say:

There are several key problems with management by reference points, particularly the *often large uncertainty* in actual stock size, and *even larger uncertainty* in unfished biomass. While some... have argued we need to move away from reference points, they are, at present, a common feature of assessment and management (emphasis added).

Thus, in spite of their apparent scientific certitude as management objectives, reference points often include "large uncertainty" in knowledge of stock sizes, and the councils have not, by the use of BRPs, escaped from that continuing problem. Nor do reference points address the social objectives of management identified by The Task Force and the National Research Council as the primary purposes of fisheries management.

BRPs have become the *de facto* objectives of groundfish management in New England, displacing the congressionally mandated objective of Optimum Yield. In the mid 1980s Anthony Calio, then the Administrator of NOAA, commissioned a report for recommendations to overhaul MFCMA in view of apparent failures of fisheries management (CFN September 1986:15). A key and highly controversial recommendation was to divide responsibilities between NMFS and the councils; NMFS would set the quotas (or OYs) and the councils would allocate the quotas among the segments of the fishing industry; who can fish and how much they can take, and who cannot. NMFS would have the relatively easy job; the councils would have the tough ones. And note that by setting quotas, NMFS, and not the councils, would in effect determine the objective of management, and that objective may or may not be OY as intended by Congress. The Calio recommendations were not implemented at the time because of strenuous objections to the idea of separating two interrelated processes or components of management. But by the incorporation of BRPs into the New England groundfish plan in recent years, the Calio recommendations seem to have come to pass, whether intended or not, whether consciously or not. And this reality seems to have come about unnoticed. In a major fisheries conference in March 2005, there were calls by those apparently unaware of what has in fact happened for a congressional amendment to MFCMA requiring the separation of NMFS and council responsibilities - NMFS to set science-based quotas and the councils to allocate the permitted catch of fish among fishermen (Crockett 2005).

Amendment 13 to the groundfish plan contains eighteen BRPs for biomass targets intended to achieve MSY for each of eighteen stocks of fish (CFN January 2004(8A). These are the objectives of the plan. We have already noted two problems associated with the concept of MSY; first, that it is of very questionable scientific validity, and, second, assuming it were a valid concept, few fisheries scientists and probably no ecologists believe that it is possible to achieve MSY for all species of a community or system at the same time. "It is energetically impossible to simultaneously maximize yield for multiple species" (Link 2002:20). William Overholst (1985:252), an NMFS scientist, wrote, "the maximum harvest of marine groundfish complexes, when based strictly on single-species criteria, may be unattainable because of techno-logical interactions in the fishery and the additional biological complexity of the exploited assemblage of fishes." These are fairly obvious difficulties with this approach to multispecies management. But there is another, deeper, and more subtle difficulty here. It has to do with the fundamental nature of organization of natural systems, including ecosystems, and it has to do with the identification of management objectives.

Howard Pattee, a biophysicist, explored the nature of complex biological and social structures (which fisheries and fisheries management surely are), and he noted that the description and explanation of such structures require two different kinds of methodologies - "two formally incompatible modes of description" (Pattee 1978:198). By way of a simple example, the physiology of humans (which surely are complex structures and functions) may be explained by blood chemistry or nerve regulations of hormones and the like, but the behavior of whole humans cannot be explained solely by such physical and chemical dynamics; they can only be explained in combination with a different kind of regulator such as parental or societal influences or constraints. At another level, a regional or national economy is explained by the dynamics of supply of raw materials, manufacturing output, money supply, transportation networks, and similar infrastructural issues. The economy is also explained by less tangible issues such as consumer confidence and societal or political purposes. Because two *kinds* of description are necessary, the inference is that complex structures consist of two kinds of phenomena; Pattee calls them structure and function, but he notes that there are other ways of expressing this basic distinction, such as "the program and the hardware, or the policy and implementation, however one may choose to express this basic distinction" (Pattee 1978:192). Pattee calls this need for two modes of explanation "complementarity," and he urges that it "is a fundamental requirement for explanatory models of social and biological systems"...."Explanation of biological systems must describe both structure and function" (Pattee 1978:191, 195). Without recognition of this necessity for two modes of description or explanation, he argues, our understanding of, and presumably management of, complex systems may likely fail.

We suggest that reliance solely on BRPs for management of fisheries systems is such a failure. BRPs are a numerical characterization of fish stocks under certain conditions. In Amendment 13 they are also used as a *de facto* statement of purpose or objective or function of the biological and socio-economic system that is the fisheries in the NEFMC plan. The council relies upon only one mode of description, that of BRPs, for its explanation of both structure and function or objective of the socio-economic and biological dimensions of the fisheries system and its plan for that system. The complementarity or two different modes of description called for by Pattee as essential for systems understanding is lacking, which is to say that the council plan relying solely on BRPs cannot be comprehensive. The council needs once again to address the question of its purpose or objective, taking into account the social and economic considerations that Congress intended to be considered in determining Optimum Yield and which The Task Force and the National Research Council stated are the primary considerations of fisheries management. Such a clearly stated objective or purpose or function of the plan would provide that second mode of description - Pattee's "complementarity" - necessary for full explanation and consideration of the system under the council's jurisdiction and is the council's responsibility.

9) Fishing Technologies

There are three common methods of taking groundfish off New England - gill nets, long-lines with hooks, and otter trawl, but most of the vessels in New England and throughout the world use the otter trawl as the principal method to catch groundfish. The otter trawl was invented in Europe and became rather widespread in the industry about one hundred years ago. Because a lot of power is necessary to tow the trawl over the bottom, the concept was only practical after engines were introduced into the fishing fleet. The otter trawl is essentially a large net bag that is towed close to or on the bottom of the ocean. The entrance to the bag is fitted with two "doors" or "otter boards," one on each side of the mouth of the bag, that are rigged to spread apart by water pressure as the net is towed and thus keep the entrance to the net open. The fish are caught in the rear of the bag which is called the "cod end." The net bag may be composed of several different mesh sizes. Often the forward end is of rather large mesh, a smaller mesh may be in the mid section, and the cod end may have a small mesh, the size of which may be determined by the species of fish in which the fisherman is most interested. The larger mesh in the forward end reduces the resistance of the bag to the water and thus reduces the power necessary to pull the trawl. The meshes at the forward end and in the midsection tend to guide the fish toward the cod end which retains the fish.

Regulating mesh size

By the 1930s the otter trawl was nearly universally used in the world's groundfisheries. Beginning in the 1930s and continuing in the 1940s there was increasing recognition of the need to set the mesh sizes by regulation to allow juvenile fish to escape. Too many immature fish were showing up in the catches of fisheries that were using small meshes, and there were signs of stock depletions, perhaps because of the capture of too many immature fish; juvenile fish were taken before they had had a chance to reproduce. Minimum mesh sizes were at last set by regulation in the 1950s - it was considered a major achievement that ICNAF was able to attain international agreement on standard mesh sizes - and further modifications continued through the 1970s and 1980s. In every case there was substantial opposition to the proposed regulations from fishermen who believed that the increased mesh sizes would allow too many fish to escape the nets. (Some fishermen knew better and used larger meshes, but kept their knowledge to themselves because they enjoyed a competitive advantage in the market with the fish of better quality which they landed with their larger meshes.)

Problems with fishing technologies

There are problems for management for the control of fishing mortalities inherent in all the traditional methods of catching groundfishes, whether long-lines with hooks, gillnets, or otter trawls. These problems include unwanted and often discarded and unrecorded bycatches and unquantifiable mortalities. These problems also occur with purse seines, mid-water trawls, and scallop dredges. Because most groundfish throughout the world are taken with otter trawls, we focus here on otter trawls. Their problems include the following:

- The doors are heavy structures which when towed along the bottom may disturb or injure the bottom habitat and living things upon which groundfish depend (National Research Council 1999:4).

- Fishes that escape through the meshes of the cod end may suffer injurious or lethal scale damage. In some cases this may be a serious problem.

- The appropriate mesh size, that is, the mesh that best retains mature fish and allows juveniles to escape, varies from species to species because their body proportions differ significantly. Thus there is no universally "right" mesh size.

- The "optimum" mesh size for any particular species may be a moving target as the body proportions of a species vary depending upon their state of nutrition.

- The escapement of juveniles from, or the retention of adults in, the cod end is less than perfect even with an "optimum" mesh size; some juveniles are always retained and some adults always escape. In heavily fished fisheries this is a significant problem.

- Bycatches were a problem the council struggled with at great length.

Worldwide, it is estimated (Alverson et al. 1994) that the bycatch may be as much as one third of the total weight of fish landed and sold, or something like 27 *million* tons. The National Research Council (1999:41) stated that "The magnitude of discard mortality and unobserved fishing mortality could be important factors contributing to global overfishing and undesirable ecological changes." Rothschild, Sharov and Lambert (1997:142) wrote that "the use of gears, such as trawls, that catch many species and sizes of fish accentuates the bycatch-discard problem, which is a major one for single-species management. Bycatch and discards can account for major portions of the fish removed from a stock, but they are notoriously difficult to estimate accurately."

Some bycatches have been reduced in recent years (NRC 1999:82) in part by research into the behavior of fish as they encounter and react to trawls, and by appropriate modifications of trawls. Significant, even dramatic, reductions of bycatches of scup and cod were observed in research trials in the yellowtail fisheries (CFN November 2001:1B). But a different configuration would be necessary to increase the escapement of yellowtail from a net intended for cod. Or of haddock in a cod fishery... Undoubtedly further refinements will be found that improve selectivity of trawls, but we suggest that given the wide variety of possible species mixes that are routinely encountered in the New England multispecies fisheries there may be diminishing returns in this approach to the problem. A recent workshop (Anon. 2004:7) noted "urgent priorities for reducing bycatch in the Northeast Region," but suggested implicitly that fine-tuning by itself of the otter trawl would be insufficient for that purpose: "Improvement in the current situation is not likely to occur without the development of a stronger culture of stewardship from within the industry....[and] Meaningful reduction in bycatch will require addressing the over-capacity issue."

In 1980 the question was asked in the council, what happens if cod in the Gulf of Maine or on Georges Bank are closed but haddock fishing continues? The answer was dramatically clear in October 2005. Maine fishermen claimed (rightly) that "excessive catch rates of cod or flounder were mixed in with the haddock catch, which resulted in an early shutdown of access to the area with a mere fraction of available haddock brought to the dock....In short... only 7 percent of the available haddock has been landed" (*Portland Press Herald*, October 12, 2005;A9).

It is not a solution to suggest that groundfish be harvested only by long-lines with hooks, for example, to avoid the problems of otter trawls. Some fishermen do very well with this method, but there are commercially important species that do not take hooks and so would be eliminated from commercial landings. And such a regulation would certainly increase fishing pressure on species that do take hooks. Hook fishing, also, has its own problems. An unknown number of fish are lost from the hooks, presumably injured, and the mortality among them is not known.

Gill nets do not have the problems of otter trawls or hooks, but they have other significant problems. Many nets are lost but may continue to drift along the bottom and trap and kill fish. Gill nets may thus contribute in a significant but unquantifiable way to fishing mortality.

We do not wish to be misunderstood by our summary of problems with fishing gear in general and the otter trawl in particular. We are not calling for a ban on these gear types. We do not propose that they be outlawed. They catch most of the marine fishes of the world and we expect they will continue to do so for years to come. Indeed, there are no practical substitutes or alternatives to them at this time. A ban on their use would cripple the world supply of fish protein in increasing demand for health and nutritional needs for the people of the world. But we do believe it is important to recognize the problems inherent in traditional gear and how the problems of conventional fishing gear contribute to the difficulties of management, particularly, of mixed-species fisheries. It would be misdirecting criticisms to condemn managers for failures to manage fish mortalities that arise from problems inherent in fishing technologies. We also believe that it is reasonable and important to think about trying to develop alternative methods of fishing that do not have the problems inherent in the existing technologies. If we do not try to conceive of efficient and benign methods of fishing we shall never make the necessary improvements.

Developing alternative technologies

We suggest that a serious effort is needed to consider the development of a *new* concept for harvesting fish. More than thirty years ago the world-renowned marine biologist Gunnar Thorson (1971:213) stated: "There is an urgent need to devise new and improved methods of fishing, and not to depend on conventional methods." There are reasons to believe that a new concept could be developed. It would be based upon the fact that *all* organisms (plants and animals) respond characteristically to a variety of sensory stimuli. Gunnar Thorson (1971:232) reported that years ago fish had been observed to be attracted to Strauss waltzes played from a hydrophone suspended in the sea. Thorson (1971:231) commented on "how much the schooling of fish depends on light, *but most fish react only to a very narrow part of the spectrum which is 'optimal' for them*" (emphasis added). Thorson also reported that out of sixty species of fish investigated off New England, fifty-six produce sound. Very likely such sound production has meaning for the species. Thorson (1971:232) wrote: "within a few years we may create new and profitable fishing methods by attracting fish shoals with recordings of their own sounds." Fisheries biologists recently learned that flatulence is a significant signal for herring. And experiments with electricity on Georges Bank "have shown that the catch of cod and haddock were unaffected but that with certain other species, such as whiting, the yield increased four- to eightfold" (Thorson 1971:233). Light of various wavelengths or frequencies, electrical impulses, chemical stimuli, odors, sound, or combinations of these undoubtedly attract, or repel, fish characteristically by species.

It is also likely that such stimuli may also be specific among the sexes and the juveniles and adults of a species. There is good reason, based upon natural selection, to take this possibility seriously. In the process of evolution, organisms adapt to or become selected for such sensory stimuli or signals as a way to prevent interbreeding and to preserve the separation of species. Similarly, there are undoubtedly signals that attract the sexes for breeding or repel them at other times to insure, for example, that males do not cannibalize their young. And juveniles also may respond to signals that separate them from cannibalistic adults. Such signals may serve other vital life processes.

There is, then, the possibility to differentially attract or repel species, ages, or sexes that we wish to catch or conserve without the numerous problems inherent in traditional technologies. And given our considerable undersea capabilities in detecting and generating a variety of signals and stimuli, it would appear practical to develop the technology to support and implement this concept.

Studies were in fact underway within NMFS in the 1970s on these questions of sensory-based fish behavior. Because of budget cuts within the agency they were discontinued, being considered of "low priority." If they had been continued, it is possible that by now they would have reached the point of practical application for fishing and for management. We believe that a serious consideration of this concept would make clear the desirability of a renewed research effort to identify the relevant signals for cod, and for haddock, and for other species of interest.

It is probable that, with our existing knowledge of signals in the sea, we could readily develop a "black box" that could generate a series or hierarchy of sensory signals that could attract or repel fish as appropriate. The appropriate signals would be programmed for the intended species of capture. By a hierarchy of signals we mean, for example, first a signal specific to attract yellowtail flounders only; then a subsignal to repel juvenile yellowtails, and a third subsignal to repel spawning yellowtails. We suspect such an arrangement or programming of signals would present no insuperable challenges to the capabilities of our electronics and communications industries - provided biologists had identified the appropriate signals for the species of interest.

Fishermen would find concentrations of their target species by their usual ever-more efficient electronic fish-finding devices. The harvesting device itself would perhaps be a kind of trap set on or near the bottom, and fitted with the stimuli-generating device and with a particle- (fish-) counting device, set by the management agency, that would automatically close the trap when an appropriate amount of fish were taken.

By this technology it would be possible for fishermen to catch "small-mesh" fish in "large-mesh" areas without unwanted or illegal bycatches of regulated species. With such a new concept of harvesting technology it would be possible to truly harvest or protect fish selectively by species, age, and sex; to control effort; to eliminate unwanted bycatches, discards, high-grading, scale damage; and all the unintended consequences of traditional quotas applied to otter trawls: in fact, to *manage* fisheries.

10) Controlling Effort?

The heart and soul of fisheries management as is appropriate for fully- or overly-developed fisheries such as those in New England, for example, is control of effort, that is, the time and energy spent in trying to catch fish. The purpose, of course, is to control, limit, or manage the mortality of fish caused by fishing. There are other causes of fish mortalities, such as predation, diseases, or old age, but there is little managers can do about these; in fact, it is extremely difficult even to estimate the percentages of death caused by these natural factors which may vary significantly from year to year. The natural variations in strengths of year classes of fish is a universally recognized and little understood phenomenon. Fisheries scientists must make estimates of recruitment and natural mortality in their mathematical calculations of population dynamics, but the estimates may be little more than guesses.

In some fisheries there may be primary considerations other than effort control, such as development of catching gear that is appropriate for that fishery or of markets, but in any well-developed fishery effort control becomes the paramount issue because what we really mean by control of effort is control of the amount of fish taken, or fishing mortality.

Elusive control of effort

Effective control of fishing mortality is undoubtedly difficult to achieve. It is hard to point to more than a very few developed fisheries throughout the world that are under truly effective effort control. And that of course is the reason for the "world fisheries crisis," in the words of the United Nations. For lack of effective control, so many stocks of fish worldwide are seriously depleted.

There are those who, without being aware of the debates or actions of NEFMC as detailed in its minutes, might conclude that the apparent lack of effective effort control in New England fisheries is just because the managers are in the pocket of the industry, or are negligent in their responsibilities, or prefer to "dither" rather than make tough decisions. This perception is perhaps the reason for so many lawsuits now demanding the attention of fisheries regulators and diverting them from focusing on the real problems of management. For that reason, such lawsuits impede progress in fisheries management.

The fact that the goal of effort control or mortality control is so elusive around the world ought to suggest that it is not a simple problem. Indeed, the terms *effort* and *control* may mean many things to many people. They may be used in management discussions with little agreement on their meaning among the participants, and that lack of agreement may not be recognized by the participants themselves in the discussions. For example, *effort* to some might mean days fished at sea by a vessel, or it might mean the actual numbers of hours with a net on the bottom compounded by the horsepower of the vessel, or it might mean the number of fish landed in port. Or it might mean the combined capabilities of a fishing fleet working on a particular stock. Unless the discussion is very specific, the participants could have very different ideas in mind. This does not contribute to progress.

Unintended consequences

It is true that management discussions do focus on a particular tactic for controlling effort, but some participants may be skeptical or opposed to that particular tactic, and perhaps for good reason. Every proposal for control of effort put forth in the first ten years of NEFMC stimulated extended discussions exploring the probability of its efficacy as well as its limitations, short-comings, and probable and often adverse unintended consequences. The discussions always included consideration of who would benefit from the tactic under discussion and who would not. There were winners and losers with every proposal. And the council had the obligation, under National Standard 4 of MFCMA, [60] of managing with equity among harvesters; a management plan by law shall not discriminate among fishermen. But the reality is that almost any significant management measure does discriminate. A simple catch quota, for example, automatically favors larger vessels that can fish in almost any weather and in any location and make their catch before the quota is taken. A catch quota may thereby favor construction of larger vessels with all-weather capability and thereby exacerbate the problem of excess fishing capacity.

Quotas

With every proposal there was skepticism among council members of the likely effectiveness in truly controlling effort for the purpose of increasing the biomass of the fish. Simple quotas by trip, for example, almost surely meant that fish caught in excess of the quota would be thrown away, unreported and wasted. They almost guaranteed "high-grading" whereby less valuable fish would be discarded until the quota was made up of the most valuable fish. Quotas encouraged the practice of late night landings - "midnight riders" - when enforcement officers were elsewhere, or of "split trips" whereby part of the catch would be unloaded at one port in which a dealer might be amenable to the suggestion that he need not record all the fish landed at his dock, while the rest of the catch would be unloaded and properly recorded in the fishing vessel's home port. And quotas encouraged the mislabeling of fish species in the catch so that regulated species, such as haddock, might be recorded as

---

[60] National Standard 4 says "Conservation and management measures shall not discriminate between residents of different states. If it becomes necessary to allocate or assign fishing privileges among various United States fishermen, such allocation shall be A) fair and equitable to all such fishermen; B) reasonably calculated to promote conservation; and C) carried out in such manner that no particular individual, corporation of other entity acquires an excessive share of such privileges."

white hake, for example. These are not hypothetical possibilities. The council had ample knowledge that such practices occurred, in fact, as a result of its regulations. Such illegal practices, of course, had their price. The fisherman involved in such deception could not expect the fair market value for the misrepresented species. And that undervalued fish entering the market would depress the price paid to law-abiding fishermen who were thus penalized for their compliance with the regulations and who thereby became opposed to the regulations with which they had tried to comply. These well-known consequences undermined the credibility of the managers and the management process. And this deception undermined the scientific process involved in estimating the status of the stocks. NMFS at one point published the statement in the Federal Register that the practice of misreporting, induced by the quotas, had so distorted the reported landings statistics, a part of the stock assessment process, that they could no longer be used by the assessment scientists. The scientists were thus inadvertently deprived by the regulations of a significant component of their assessment procedures upon which the managers depended.

Quarterly or annual quotas also meant that there would be a race among fishermen to catch their share before the total quota was taken and the fishery were closed. This lead to many problems; fishing in unsafe weather conditions, gluts in the market, disruption of market and distribution systems, the encouragement of imports when the domestic fishery was closed, wildly fluctuating prices to fishermen and consumers as the landings fluctuated. All these problems were in fact experienced. Much of the extended and agonizing council discussions were directed toward avoiding or correcting these kinds of problems created by its early implementation of quotas, whether by trip or by season or by year. And Weber (2002:87) noted: "The limited ability of NMFS and the U.S. Coast Guard to enforce quotas encouraged widespread misreporting and poaching, further undermining confidence in the new management system."

In reviewing the history of the New England fisheries in the

1960s and 1970s, Margaret Dewar (1983:125) noted that problems that NEFMC experienced with quotas had been experienced previously under ICNAF:

> quotas gave an advantage to large, distant-water vessels because the larger boats could fish in any weather... They would leave nothing of the quota for United States fishermen....Fishermen and boat owners objected to throwing away dead fish and promoting waste in order to stay within the ICNAF catch limits (Dewar 1983:125-6).

Dewar also noted that under ICNAF vessels fishing on other species were allowed an "incidental" catch of regulated species which could exceed the total directed catch of the U.S. fleet. The U.S. fisheries officials involved with ICNAF apparently learned nothing from the lessons about problems inherent in quotas and so the problems were repeated under MFCMA.

> While ICNAF's dilemma offered a rich opportunity for learning about the pitfalls of certain styles of fishery management, few of the groups involved drew these lessons. ICNAF's problems, however, may have had as much to do with management strategy as with the foreign-domestic conflict. Failure to understand this on the part of the industry, their spokesmen, and NMFS officials meant domestic fishery management would re-enact many of the ICNAF battles. The National Marine Fisheries Service, charged with writing interim fishery management plans while the council began operations, used ICNAF's approach as a blueprint (Dewar 1983:147).

Let us recapitulate some of the problems inherent in quotas.

A quota is an extremely blunt instrument that can result in chronic and sometimes massive discards - dumping at sea - of marketable fish. And such dumped fish will frequently be injured or dead. A constant complaint from fishermen is that they find it sickening to kill good market fish and throw them overboard. This is not limited to otter trawl fishermen. Hook fishermen, gillnetters, and seiners have the same problem.

Quotas have resulted in market distortions that have caused markets to disappear, and destroyed infrastructure of the industry. [61] Quotas cause excessive fishing pressure on stressed stocks. As this was written - February 28, 2004 - the squid fleet had been warned that the quarterly quota for squid would be closed in about a week. Most of the displaced boats would then turn to groundfishing. They might do something else, but they were apprehensive that if they do not use their groundfishing days (DAS) they would lose them - use it or lose it - so that because of the squid closure they apply additional pressure to the groundfish stocks.

Frequently quotas cause inefficient operations. Over recent two or three seasons a southern New England day-boat fleet of draggers has high-graded to their two- or three-hundred-pound daily quota of fluke, then come in at noon as before. They try to go every day regardless of weather. The cheaters unload this $2-$4-per-pound fish in the middle of the night. We know of no instance when enforcement officers have been on the docks other than normal business hours during the day. Quotas have resulted in violators being rewarded and honest fishermen being penalized through poor enforcement and misreporting.

While the council struggled to react to these problems, there was continuing uncertainty that the regulations were in fact controlling effort and mortality and saving fish. Indeed, from the continuing and reliable reports of illegal fishing and landings practices, there was reason to believe that they were not. But the council could not be sure if they were or were not. The only sure (objective?) evidence would be from the scientific assessments, but there is

---

[61] A complaint in the winter of 2004 in Maine was that very limited open seasons for shrimp fishing have shut off investment in processing capacity to the point that there is a limited market for the catch that was permissible and landed.

inherently great uncertainty in those estimates which were further distorted, as we noted, by the effects of the quotas. The assessments have very little predictive value, and because of the methodology involved they may be perhaps as much as fifty percent in error. The accuracy increases as the assessment for a particular year class recedes in time, but the condition of a stock five years ago is of little interest to a manager today. The fact is that the benefits of any effort control could escape detection on short-term basis because of the real-time uncertainties of the assessment methods. The council had no real-time measure of the effectiveness of its intended effort-control quotas.

We may note in passing that even a *closure* of a fishery may not control effort or fishing mortality. In May 1981 the Regional Administrator of NMFS informed the council "that during past yellowtail closures landings were *higher* than during times when there were no closures" (emphasis added) (Pierce MS 1982:92).

Fishery reserves

The council has always used closed areas - or "fishery reserves" as they are now called - to reduce or prevent fishing effort on juvenile or spawning fish. More recently, closed areas have been designated to try to reduce overall fishing effort on stressed stocks. The closed areas off New England have become ever more complicated and of greater extent, but "the value of such closures and reserves remains generally untested" (Auster and Shackell 1997:159). To be effective closed areas must be based upon considerable knowledge of the biology and habitat preferences of the species of interest. The impact upon other species in the area should be considered, and there is concern that the fishing effort that is diverted out of a closed area is then concentrated and increased upon fishes in open areas. It was for this reason Canadians considered but decided against a closed area for groundfish off southern Labrador in the 1970s. There is a Catch-22 here. A number of advocates of closed areas (e. g., Pauly and MacLean 2003) believe that to be effective they must be large. But the larger the closed areas, the greater the impact of displaced fishing effort upon the stocks in open areas. "the higher the fishing mortality outside the reserves and the greater the mobility of the fish, the larger the reserves would have to be to remain effective" (Auster and Shackell 1997:160). But with greater knowledge and trials, fishery reserves might be beneficial and a useful management tactic for the stocks, or to protect critical features of habitat although these are presently poorly understood for groundfish. Those authors wrote:

> Fisheries management is inexact because complete information about complex systems is unaffordable and partial information obtained from sampling and research can be inaccurate or misleading. Fishery reserves offer a buffer against uncertainty. A system of no-, limited-, or full-fishing zones can become a cornerstone of fisheries management.

> In the short term... closures have economic and social costs. Because the utility of reserves has yet to be demonstrated in practice, anticipated costs may inspire considerable opposition to a reserve system (Auster and Shackell 1997:165).

Limited entry

The council in its first ten years had frequently been urged by NMFS to adopt a limited entry system, of an unspecified nature, for the New England groundfish fisheries. The implication was that this was the road to real effort control or reduction. The council did not ignore that advice. In fact, it was explicit [62] that "the issue of limiting entry shall as a matter of council determined procedure be considered in all FMPs." But the council recognized that it is a controversial and extremely complicated issue with no practical example of how it might be implemented and with no

---

[62] Fishery Management Plan for the Atlantic Groundfish Fishery. Part 1: Statement of the Problem. New England Fishery Management Council Staff. Res. Doc. 79 GF 4.2. April, 1979.

unanimity of opinion as to its benefits for stocks of fish. Chris Kellogg, a staff economist and presently the Deputy Executive Director for the council, noted that limited entry could not be effective unless it was based upon data for the historical performances of vessels - which is not often available, and that there was an estimated five-year implementation procedure - hardly a timely possibility given the situation confronting the council. Indeed, MFCMA [63] required the following factors to be taken into account in any limited entry program:

1) present participation in the fishery;

2) historical fishing practices in, and dependence upon the fishery;

3) the economics of the fishery;

4) the capability of fishing vessels used in the fishery to engage in other fisheries;

5) the cultural and social framework relevant to the fishery; and

6) any other relevant consideration.

The time required to collect, prepare, and analyze this information would itself preclude timely implementation. Most likely during that time the prospect of limited entry would, as happened in 1977 and 1978, stimulate an increase in fishing permit applications. And it is apparent that much subjective judgment, inviting disputes and controversy, would be involved in considering those factors, such as what are the "economics" of the fishery, or the cultural and social framework, or other relevant considerations.

Nevertheless, the council explored the concept. It began to consider limited entry on its agenda in January 1978 and council members attended a national limited entry conference in Denver in 1978. The council participants were not convinced, based on

---

[63] MFCMA 303(b)(6)

what they had heard at the conference, of the feasibility of adopting limited entry to the New England fisheries. Their concerns were that:

1) It had not been demonstrated to help fish stocks biologically.

2) It demanded data and information that was not available.

3) None of the limited entry program described at the conference were successful in controlling effort.

Two motions at the first two council meetings early in 1979 were introduced to impose a moratorium on new entrants into the fisheries. [64] Both were defeated in fairly close votes, and council members associated with the industry were divided on the question. The council remained open to consideration of the issue and directed its staff to consider the concept as one of the various management tactics for ADF, but its deliberations always found serious problems or undesirable consequences in the concept. [65] Economists Townsend and Charles (1997:178) wrote:

> There have been two key problems with limited entry. First, most limited entry programs began as moratoria on entry after the number of participants in the fishery had already become large. Only in rare cases has government reduced the number of licenses either by revoking or buying back licenses. Second, each vessel has an incentive to expand its fishing capacity, a problem known as "capital stuffing." As a result, limited entry alone has almost never been successful in the long term at preventing economic

---

[64] Less than two years earlier a primary congressional intent underlying MFCMA was the *development* of the U.S. fishing fleet.

[65] For example, the council was urged to adopt a form of limited entry called ITQs, based upon the new experimental concept adopted in New Zealand for the Orange Ruffy fishery. Within a few years that fishery had collapsed.

overfishing.

The administrative steps in implementing a limited entry program were formidable. NMFS pointed out [66] what was necessary for approval at the federal level (CFN December 1985:6):

> 1) that the legal and administrative requirements of the MFCMA must be adhered to thoroughly in the development of any such system; 2) that the administrative and policy review network goes beyond the Councils or NMFS - through [the Department of] Commerce to OMB [Office of Management and Budget]; and 3) that the requirements of limited entry systems are defined by the MFCMA and other applicable law such as the Administrative Procedures Act, Executive Order 12291, and the Regulatory Flexibility Act must be met.

Council member Richard Allen commented (CFN December 1985:6) that "If anyone thinks they can start from here and get to there through that maze of bureaucrats and lawyers, I'd like to see it." Even the regional science director for NMFS was reported to be "an avowed opponent of limited entry, believing it would be of little benefit to either the industry or the resource" (*National Fisherman Yearbook* 1985:28).

It was fully apparent to the council that adoption of limited entry programs, even if feasible, would change fundamentally the social, cultural, and economic characteristics of the New England groundfisheries. But a generally agreed-upon purpose of the council was to try to preserve traditional New England fisheries based largely on family-owned vessels; the council believed that was an important part of its job. Further, it was perceived that limited entry in one fishery must inevitably and profoundly affect

---

[66] Limited Entry and Fisheries Management under the MFCMA, a draft paper by Michael Ohrbach, summarized in National Fisherman, August 1985:16-18.

all of the region's complicated and interrelated fisheries, not just those to which it was specifically applied, but in ways that no one could adequately or accurately predict. In fact, The Task Force (Hennemuth et al. 1980:3) had warned explicitly that 'limited entry' might be aimed at reducing fishing effort, but in choosing this method, one implies that the social or economic consequences of it are also objectives of the plan" - which with the New England council they were not.

The council was aware that Canadians had had poor experiences with limited entry programs. Next door to New England, "in the Canadian Maritimes, boat quotas [a form of limited entry] were seen as 'the bright new hope' in management when they were implemented in 1976," *Commercial Fisheries News* (July 1985:7) quoted Joe Gough, formerly editor and publisher of *Canadian Fishing Report*: "Boat quotas so far have brought little real reduction in the fleet or for that matter in the size of replacement boats." Apparently there was blatant cheating and misreporting among Bay of Fundy herring seiners. Gough stated: "Despite a tough government clamp down, cheating remains widespread and widely known... How much they overfish is anyone's guess; sometimes you hear suggestions of 50%....The question is often asked: if it's so hard to enforce individual quotas for 50 or 60 seiners, how can it ever happen for hundreds or thousands of boats?"

Finally, in 1986, under continuing and increasing pressure from NMFS to adopt limited entry, by a formal and nearly unanimous [67] vote the council *directed* (note that it did not request) NMFS to provide the council with specific recommendations on effort controls and catch controls with regard to the multispecies groundfish plan for council consideration. [68] NMFS never responded to that directive. A council staff memo [69] later noted

---

[67] We believe the NMFS Regional Administrator abstained.

[68] council minutes, February 11-12, 1986

[69] pwc/Council/FMPProcess.4.25.95

that "NMFS has backed away from advocating IFQs", a form of limited entry.

There is another phenomenon within the industry that bears upon the question of effort control within limited entry programs or other tactics. This is the ever-changing efficiency of fishing vessels. A substantial increase in efficiency is very apparent. The design of otter trawlers, particularly of stern trawlers, of the 1980s was remarkably better than those of the 1950s or 1960s. The catching efficiency of nets and towing gear was improved. The vessels of the 1980s had electronic navigation and fish-finding equipment that was far superior to those of earlier years. This evolution of efficiency is a normal part of the development of any fishing fleet. Increased efficiency was an original congressional intent for MFCMA. One would expect it to become accelerated under the pressure of stringent regulatory controls; the industry and its suppliers would react to restrictions on fishing effort by trying to make the vessels ever more efficient. Chris Kellogg, staff economist for the New England council, estimated that New England vessels increased their efficiency by ten percent per year over a five-year period in the late 1960s and early 1970s. Other economists estimated a rather smaller but nevertheless significant rate of increase of efficiencies worldwide; "the rate of increase in fishing power resulting from technological improvements has averaged 4.4 percent annually since 1965" (NRC 1999:28). Writing of New England vessels, Hennessey and Healey (2000:203) noted:

> By 1991, vessel numbers had declined by about 20%... [But} All evidence indicates that the efficiency of individual fishing vessels increased substantially during both the quota management and indirect management phases....Thus the 20% decline in [New England] vessel numbers was more than offset by increases in vessel efficiency.

Thus vessels became significantly more efficient under the pressure of regulations intended to restrict their effort and their catches.

It is ironic that Shelley et al. (1996:235), who were critical of the council for not effectively controlling fishing mortality, wrote:

> While there can be no question that the "open fisheries" in New England exacerbated the capital inflow problem in the groundfish fishery, accelerating capitalization in the form of technological improvements occurs in "closed fisheries" as well and has the same practical effect as far as fishing effort and mortality is concerned.

There was nothing the council could do to limit that ever-increasing technological efficiency. One would expect that that increase has continued. This, of course, is one reason why the currently fashionable limitation on "days-at-sea" may not be a very effective *long-term* control on effort. It almost certainly stimulates ways of increasing efficiency, fishing power, and fishing skills within the limited days at sea. Vessels that previously might need 100 days at sea per year could conceivably now fish profitably on seventy days per year. "In 2002, the Council reduced the number of days-at-sea... fishermen were allowed to fish by nearly 40%, but Georges Bank cod catch actually went up by more than 15%" (Crockett 2005:195). In 2006 the council was of the opinion that "days-at-sea" is not an effective control on effort and it began a search for a new strategy.

Buyback programs

Let us consider another facet of this problem. We quoted Townsend and Charles (1997:178), above, that a key problem with limited entry is that only rarely have governments accompanied such programs with revocations or buyback of licenses or (we add) of vessels. But buyback programs also have their limitations. In 1995 the federal government spent nearly $25 million "buying out" seventy-nine vessels out of a total of 1793 permits in the New England fleet. The purpose was to reduce the size of the fleet and thus reduce the effort or fishing mortality on the stocks. The target of the program was to remove about ten percent of the New England fleet. But consider the ratio of fishing power (i. e., roughly the number of vessels) to stock sizes. Let us assume for the argument that about 1,000 vessels were responsible for reducing the haddock population, for example, to ten percent of its size in the 1950s which was a healthy stock size. (In fact the U.S. haddock landings were reduced to about six percent of the average landings of 1950-66.) Let us also suppose that that stock size, for sake of the argument, was 100,000 tons. Thus the ratio of 1,000 vessels to 100,000 tons may be compared to the reduced fleet of 900 vessels and the depleted stock of 10,000 tons. Granted the fleet was reduced somewhat in size, but the result would have been a nine-fold net increase in relative fishing power (assuming the unlikely case that vessels had stayed constant in fishing efficiency) upon the seriously reduced stock size - not a promising method of controlling effort. But this is a theoretical scenario.

After describing what actually happened in the New England buyback program, designed not by the council but by NMFS, Weber (2002:208), a former NMFS employee, concluded: "In the end, the buyback program in New England had little effect on the fishing capacity of the New England groundfish fleet. The program did demonstrate some of the difficulties in designing effective buyback programs"

Fishing industry members made a new effort in 2006 to devise a buyback program, but early in 2007 that effort was abandoned because of its complexities and other reasons (CFN May 2007:9A).

Individual Fishing Quotas

A currently popular answer to the question of effective effort control is the concept of Individual Fishing Quotas (IFQs). The basic concept is also known as Individual Transferable Quotas

(ITQs), and there are other names for the general concept. [70] There are of course a number of variations on the general theme of IFQs, but in short and simplistic terms an IFQ is a program in which only so many entities (people, vessels, or corporations) would be permitted to take fish from a particular stock or population, and the amount of fish that each could take would be strictly limited and specified beforehand. Under IFQs, each entity has the right to catch its allocated amount of fish. The concept is intended not only to limit effort, but also to create a vested interest on the part of participants in conservation of the resource; that is to say, "ownership" would induce stewardship. (We do not enter here into the ongoing debate whether IFQs can or should convey essentially exclusive property ownership rights over hitherto publicly owned fisheries resources.) There are now approximately 125 quota management programs in about eighteen countries around the world. Only four are in the U.S.; none in New England. Iceland and New Zealand are in the forefront of developing IFQs for their fisheries. Dierdre Boelke, on the staff of NEFMC, has looked carefully at IFQs and considers that indeed some programs have been beneficial in improving *economic* efficiency of a number of fisheries, but that there is little evidence that they have improved *biological* conditions of the stocks. (A notorious example is that under an early IFQ program, the Orange Ruffy fishery of New Zealand collapsed.) In particular, Boelke is of the opinion that the IFQ concept is not practical for the complex and diverse groundfish fisheries of New England. A document [71] prepared in 1995 by the council staff noted that "groundfish fisheries and resources are in *dire straits* almost everywhere in the world including those nations that have managed with limited entry, IFQs, quotas and fishing mortality targets" (emphasis added). As recently as 2004, an independent report (Anon. MS 2004) noted that "overfishing in the form of exceeding the total allowable catch can still occur under IFQs,"

---

[70] The recent (2006) amendments to MFCMA refer to the concept as LAPPs (Limited Access Privilege Programs).

[71] pwc/Council/FMPProcess.4.25.95

and "IFQs can increase bycatch because fishermen often keep only the most economically valuable fish (this is known as high-grading)." The report contains a number of references to deleterious biological impacts of IFQs; e.g.,

- "political pressure has led to the setting of TACs (total allowable catch) beyond maximum sustainable yield";

- "IFQs potentially create incentives to cheat by underreporting catches and high-grading by keeping only the most economically valuable part of catches"

- "discarding of small and immature fish... and high-grading the catch seem to be serious problems in the Icelandic fishery and these problems may have escalated with ITQs"

- "ITQs do not solve the problems [bycatch, joint catch] of multispecies fisheries management and may intensify some of them".

The report also noted that IFQs significantly increase the cost of management; it reported that the government of The Netherlands is moving away from IFQs due to high management costs. It reported that fisheries failures occurred in three species under IFQs in New Zealand, and that after ten years under IFQ management the Canadian east coast cod and groundfish populations collapsed. The report concluded "In sum, IFQs do not eliminate existing environmental problems and can actually exacerbate them." Alison Rieser (1999) also noted that IFQ programs would seem to work against effective management of fisheries *systems* (as contrasted with single-species management), which must be an inescapable goal. (Because this is a major issue and one of the three issues we consider of fundamental importance, we will return to consider it at length later.) As NEFMC learned the hard way, there are always unanticipated and usually undesirable consequences from complicated management schemes. The National Research Council (1999:67) noted that "Despite considerable study, there remain major uncertainties in how fishers... will respond to such management options as individual transferable quotas."

Let us consider briefly some of the practical problems of applying an IFQ program to the New England groundfish fishery. The first problem is that of defining the fishery; who is a groundfish fishermen? That is simple for a large stern trawler working year-round on Georges Bank. It is not so simple for an inshore, small-boat fisherman who fishes part-time for regulated groundfish and who also may fish seasonally for unregulated groundfish, or for lobsters, or scallops, or shrimp.

> Because fish behavior and weather conditions so sharply constrain their work, inshore fishermen need to be able to move quickly and without too much expense from one fishery to another. Catching different kinds of fish and shellfish frequently requires changes in gear. Inshore fishermen use otter trawls or line trawls to catch cod, haddock, and flounder; but they need otter trawls with finer mesh to catch whiting, dredges to harvest scallops, seines to capture herring, and traps to bring in lobsters (Dewar 1983:17).

This is not an uncommon situation in Maine, for example - or was prior to the imposition of stringent groundfish regulations. Fishermen practiced such a diverse fishing pattern for the excellent reason that various species were only seasonally available to them, and because the practice provided a buffer against the natural variations of numbers that were common within their experience; by this strategy fishermen avoided species in low numbers and thus relieved excessive fishing pressure upon them. Now, if such a fisherman were to be included within an IFQ program and thereby given exclusive rights to regulated ground-fish, then he should not expect to continue fishing for other species that are not groundfish - shrimps, scallops or lobsters - in competition with fishermen for those species who are not in the IFQ program. He could not, or should not, enjoy a favored position compared with other fishermen who took those species but did not take groundfish. The IFQ fishermen, thus, would be confined to one or a few species; his flexibility in the face of natural variations in stock sizes or availabilities would be diminished or lost and he would be vulnerable to normal variabilities of regulated species. He would be forced to continue to fish on species reduced in numbers, thus exacerbating the problem of a declining resource.

Consider the question of deciding which species would define a groundfish IFQ program. The council initially included fifteen species, because of their biological and economic interactions, in its ADF plan with the expectation of including additional species. This number of species would mean that practically every vessel in New England that set a trawl or gillnet or fished with hooks could be included in the program. This is hardly controlling fishing mortality on overfished stocks, nor are all the groundfish in New England considered overfished. The presumably controlled fishing effort or fishing mortality of an IFQ program clearly would be dissipated by the practical difficulties of defining the limits of such a scheme. NMFS in 1995 had ceased to urge the council to adopt IFQs for the New England fishery, but in 2005 NMFS was again promoting the concept.

Single-species effort control

Consider the case of controlling effort in a "simple" single-species fishery such as the Maine lobster fishery. This is a fishery in which, in theory, it ought to be easy to control mortality simply by limiting licenses and by limiting trap numbers. But Maine's fisheries department has acknowledged how difficult it is to figure out how to reduce effort in a way that is equitable across all license holders (CFN October 2004:3B). For example, the existing state trap limit program includes a provision for "entry ratios" whereby a new license is issued only when between two and five licenses, depending upon the region or "lobster zone" of the coast, are retired. This provision was intended to reduce the numbers of fishermen and traps in the water. But "the various schemes [i. e. entry ratios] along the coast don't seem to have any effect" (*Fishermen's Voice*, February 2005:9). The report went on to state that "even if a zone goes to a 1:5 ratio, it would be decades before there is a reduction of effort." The fact of the matter is that effort within a fixed trap limit can increase by several means; by hauling traps more frequently, by boats with bigger engines and therefore greater speed able to cover greater fishing areas within a given time, by ever-more precise electronic devices pinpointing lobster concentrations and reducing searching time for trap locations, by more efficient lobster traps (it is increasingly recognized that conventional traps are not efficient in *retaining* lobsters), and by noncompliance with regulations. It is believed by some enforcement officers that in some parts of the Gulf of Maine there may be eighty percent *non*compliance with regulations. While it is believed by enforcement officers that in well-patrolled fishing waters there is probably eighty percent compliance, the implied twenty percent noncompliance means that there could be as many as half a million *illegal* traps adding to fishing mortality of the lobster population. This number of potentially illegal traps is in excess of all the traps that were fished each year in the Maine lobster fishery from 1880 to 1954. The Lobster Advisory Council in 2004 concluded that Maine's complicated lobster effort management program is not working due to a build up of traps and an inability to get rid of "latent" effort (CFN October 2004:3B; *Fishermen's Voice*, November 2004:25). None of this gives much confidence that there is effective control on effort or fishing mortality even in a single-species fishery in which such controls ought to be relatively easy to implement and enforce. The problems would be magnified in more complicated fisheries. The National Research Council (1999:121) observed that in general "Fishers adapt ingeniously to regulations designed to reduce fishing capacity, by improving technology, fishing 'smarter' or harder, and modifying their techniques."

Search for effective effort control

Considering the recognized and substantial deficiencies of these various effort control strategies and tactics, it is a not unreasonable conclusion, therefore, that perhaps we do not in fact know how to effectively control fishing mortality in a variety of simple or complex fisheries. Ragnar Arnason, a professor of economics at the University of Iceland, said: "Effort reduction does not work because fishing effort has so many variables. You can always find the dimension of effort that is not constrained and is not constrainable" (Clover 2006:247). This is a significant and sobering possibility; it has profound implications for the well-being of stocks and for fisheries management. If we are proceeding on the assumption that we *do* know how to control effort - that the various effort control mechanisms currently in practice, or advocated, really control effort or mortality when in fact they do not - then our management programs are based upon a very questionable foundation. The possibility that these effort control tactics are ineffective suggests that such management programs cannot succeed - that they are bound to fail. These considerations suggest that fisheries managers do not have tools, tactics, or strategies than can effectively control fisheries mortalities. If they did, there would not be "the world fisheries crisis" as described by the United Nations.

More than thirty-five years ago the Stratton Commission (Commission on Marine Science, Engineering and Resources 1969:107) acknowledged this reality:

> As a practical matter, it is presently impossible to devise a workable program to restrict fishing effort directly. Total fishing effort is a function of many factors - the number of vessels employed; their size, power, and type of gear; the number of hours spent in fishing and the particular season and grounds fished [and, we might add, the experience of the fishermen]. To date, there is no internationally accepted unit of fishing effort, which combines all these factors. Even if there were, it would be virtually impossible to enforce direct limits on the amount of fishing, particularly the number of hours fished by vessels far from home.

We suggest, further, that existing strategies for effort control

should be critically examined within the context of the requirement of National Standard 4 that management shall not discriminate among fishermen of different regions. This is an issue that
constantly confronted and confounded the New England council
in its earliest days, and notoriously so with the development in
2003 of Amendment 13. The council then and now found that no
matter what controls it considered, one group or another of
fishermen would be disadvantaged relative to another.

Further, we suggest that a review of the efficacy of effort controls
should be in the context, also, of an intent and desire to preserve
the traditional economic and cultural context of the fisheries. The
New England council began in 1977 with general agreement that
its intent was to "restore stocks without major industry
dislocations" (Anon. MS 1977). That council purpose was at least
implicitly reinforced by several of the National Standards,
including those that prohibit discriminations among fishermen of
different regions (#4) and forbid economic allocations as a sole
purpose (#5). The 1996 amendments to MFCMA further
reinforced the council's policy with a new National Standard (#8)
that required management measures to "provide for the sustained
participation" of fishing communities and as far as practical to
"minimize adverse economic impacts on such communities." The
council, in its struggle to find effective control tactics,
encountered the reality at almost every turn that all conceivable
control tactics inevitably embodied features that were discriminatory with respect to access to the resources, led to economic
inequities, or would seriously disrupt the traditional nature of
New England's diverse, dispersed, owner-operated, small-boat
fisheries that uses a variety of gear, and that harvested across a
spectrum of species. This last characteristic has for many years
been a fishing strategy that tends to reduce effort on any one
species and improves the chances of the fleet to adapt to the
common and naturally-occurring fluctuations in the numbers of a
particular stock of fish. This is one of the reasons the council
wished to preserve the flexibility of individual vessels to shift
among species. Effort control schemes such as limited entry or
IFQs would certainly reduce if not eliminate that flexibility.

Those realities still plague council deliberations.

We regret that, unless we develop a new concept of selective fishing technologies with built-in controls on catching capacity such as that we suggested previously, we do not have a specific recommendation for explicit and effective effort control strategies or tactics. We wish we did. We strongly suggest, because of the reasons we have outlined, that assumptions of effective controls should be examined with skepticism. We suggest that there should be a formal, objective, critical, and thorough review and evaluation of the efficacy and results of various kinds of control programs - whether quotas, buybacks, fishery reserves, IFQs, days-at-sea, limited entry, and trap limits - upon the well-being of fish stocks around the world. We would then be in a better position to judge whether fine-tuning of the existing concepts would suffice, or whether it would be necessary to develop wholly new concepts for effort controls. Later we will suggest a different method for control of fishing mortality based upon a hypothesis of how ecosystems function.

11) Understanding Fisheries Systems

A multitude of species to manage

In the fall of 1976, before the New England council was officially in existence, it held several organizational and orientation meetings for its newly appointed members, most of whom, in the words of a 1995 staff memo, [72] "were new to the responsibilities of resource management... The members of the Council began a learning process that is ongoing to this time."

Scientists of NMFS identified for the council fourteen species "which were one quarter of the species that must be managed by the council." [73], [74] At an earlier meeting a senior scientist had "stressed the importance of trying to manage nine groundfish species *separately* in the future" (emphasis added). [75] In effect, NMFS advice to the council at that time was that it would have to develop *fifty-six* separate management plans and then sustain fifty-six separate management regimes. Even at that time of

---

[72] pwc/Council/FMPPROCESS.4.25.95

[73] council minutes, November 8-10, 1976

[74] A criticism (Shelley et al, 1996:236) of the council: "In New England, the interpretation of the FCMA threshold [for determining the need for management plans] has been such that management plans are not developed until the fishery is already significantly underway and already manifesting signs of biological stress." The fact, of course, is that in New England almost all the fisheries had been fully developed for years, even decades, prior to the MFCMA and the creation of the councils.

[75] council minutes, October 26, 1976

naiveté and innocence of what was to come, the council must have considered that to be an awesome task. And no one apparently noted then that such a strategy of separate management plans recommended by NMFS would have been a violation of National Standard 3 which says in part "interrelated stocks of fish shall be managed as a unit or in close coordination." Even in 1976 there should have been little doubt, as the council later stated in ADF, that many of the stocks were interrelated biologically and economically. The innocence of NMFS, also, was revealed by its assertion that so many species must be managed separately. As part of its "ongoing learning process" in the next few years the council combined eleven species, and then by the laborious amendment process added three more species, into its Northeast Multispecies Fishery Management Plan, or ADF, implemented in 1986. It had learned by hard experience that it could not hope to manage by separate plans the diverse but interrelated groundfish species of New England; that an attempt to do so would only result in a hopeless confusion of unenforceable and ineffective regulations working at cross purposes. But in reality it did not try to actively manage more than three of those fourteen species.

Early on, the council recognized that single species could not be managed in isolation. A number of developments reinforced that reality. Continuing reports of large numbers of discarded bycatches of several species was one such issue. A more fundamental reality was that a number of species that occur on the same fishing grounds would inevitably and unavoidably be taken by the otter trawl. The laborious and controversial efforts to develop the Exempted Fisheries Program (a newer version of the program is now known as the Special Access Program, SAP) was one reflection of this reality.

Even in the midst of the continuing crises created by the original groundfish plan, the council began the development of a multi-species plan with the explicit acknowledgement of unavoidable and significant biological and economic interactions among species. With the gradual evolution and modification of that Northeast Multispecies Fishery Management Plan, Amendment

13 of 2003 includes twelve species comprising twenty identifiable stocks. [76]

Moving toward systems management

The council for thirty years has been moving slowly and painfully toward at least an implicit recognition that it is trying to manage not just a number of species of fishes, but a *system* of fishes - a most significant evolution of management thinking. The council is not alone, of course, in this thinking. The Task Force (Hennemuth et al. 1980:6) stated:

> In view of the dynamic interactions in nature, a single-species approach to management is inadequate, particularly for multispecies fisheries, or where the bycatch is significant.

> To avoid the deficiencies of a single-species approach, management must address itself to the productivity and harvest potential of an entire system, *since the ecosystem in the long run has greater stability than any of its components* (emphasis added).

We will come back to this last and most significant observation; we believe it lies at the heart of successful fisheries management.

The growing recognition that it is a system that must be managed had profound implications and presented immense challenges to the council. Principal among them was the fact that no working hypothesis suggesting just what a system of marine fisheries is or how it functions was available or offered to the council. The council in fact had implicitly asked the questions, "What is a fisheries system?" and "How do we manage it?" - to which there has been no pragmatic, no *operational*, answer. There were no

---

[76] Early in 2005 the council has implemented seven (not fifty-six) management plans and has one more for hagfish in preparation.

guiding principles to which the council could turn for assistance in its attempt to manage the multispecies resources of New England. There was no scientific advice to the council on this fundamental scientific question. It was and is one of the major "unanswerable questions" to which The Task Force had confessed, although the experts on The Task Force did not raise or address the issue in terms of defining fisheries systems.

Little progress has been made in the last twenty years to answer that question even though in the last ten or so years there has emerged an extensive and rapidly growing literature on "ecosystems-based" management of fisheries. It would take a considerable effort to digest even part of that literature. From a sampling, one comes away with the impression that attempts to implement the ill-defined idea of ecosystems management would be very data-hungry, very expensive, and burdensome with an even greater complexity of analyses and regulations than has prevailed to date (e. g., Gislason et al. 2000). The concept is handicapped by the absence of a common understanding of what ecosystems-based management would be. As recently as 2004, Hilborn, Punt, and Orensanz (2004:493) noted that "Ecosystem management has remained an elusive concept that can mean vastly different things to different people." And Lee Alverson (2004:639), after reviewing some of the literature, wrote: "The concept of management using ecosystem principles is broadly endorsed by many scientists, but opinion still differs about many terms associated with the state of ecosystems, the attributes that will retain ecosystem productivity, and *principles that should guide management*....confusion about terms and concern about promoted ecological concepts [are] widespread" (emphasis added). In other words, fisheries science lacks an operational characterization of the structures and functions of ecosystems.

We, like many others, believe effective fisheries management depends upon identifying and applying ecosystems characteristics. And we address the problem identified by Alverson, that of the apparent lack of potentially practical and useful ecosystems hypotheses. We believe there is such a hypothesis, apparently not yet recognized in fisheries science, which we will outline here. An outstanding attraction of the hypothesis that we recommend is that it could greatly *simplify* effective fisheries management.

The role of yellowtail flounder in a system

As an approach to that issue, let us first consider yellowtail flounder as part of the question of understanding fisheries systems. Our purpose here is to give a concrete example of an important characteristic of marine ecosystems.

The council was advised early in 1977 that yellowtails in the area off southern New England were "severely depressed" and that no directed fishery should be permitted - that only unavoidable bycatch landings of less than 5510 pounds per trip should be permitted. In January 1978 NMFS advised the council that yellowtail landings from that area had exceeded the quota by sixty-five percent, and that, even though yellowtail landings did *not* exceed the quota in the area near and on Georges Bank, the situation there had "drastically deteriorated." In May it was noted that "extremely restrictive" limits were needed. In February 1979 NMFS reported that the yellowtail situation had not improved. In November and December the landings were reported to be very high and had exceeded the quarterly allocations. Over a year later, in March 1981, the council was informed that unrecorded yellowtail landings were much in excess of the limits.

But by May 1983, two years later, NMFS reported that new surveys suggested a significant increase in numbers of yellowtails since the rock-bottom years of the mid 1970s in spite of the apparently severe overfishing of the previous five years. Size and age composition from a 1981 survey indicated continued improvement in recruitment, although other data showed that mortality in 1980 was much higher than would be considered desirable. (Recall that we saw a similar phenomenon with Gulf of Maine cod in 1999-2001, a great increase in biomass under very high fishing mortality.) Surveys of yellowtail in 1983 indicated continued improvement in biomass - "a substantial increase in abundance" (NMFS in CFN January 1984:19) - since 1978. That conclusion was confirmed in a new report in January 1984. But a year later NMFS reported (CFN March 1985:23) that "prospects for the coming year are very poor." It noted that this "represents an abrupt reversal in the condition of this fishery." But then yellowtails enjoyed a recovery in the late 1980s and declined to very low levels in the mid-1990s. NMFS reported to the council in December 1993 that southern New England yellowtail stocks had collapsed and that there should be no fishing on those stocks. The stock numbers had improved two years later and had improved somewhat again by 2001. In reporting these results, NMFS also added, as an historical note, that the yield of the fishery had peaked in the early 1940s, collapsed in the mid-1950s, and peaked again in the late 1960s. It would seem that yellowtail flounder had experienced substantial fluctuations in numbers and biomass in the thirty-odd years before MFCMA and the heavy fishing pressures of the 1980s. Most recently, a review in 2005 of groundfish stocks through 2004 found that yellowtails off southern New England were "severely overfished." The review found that the spawning stock biomass was only ten percent of the target biomass and that the fishing mortality rate was more than twice the target rebuilding rate (CFN February 2006:1B). But in the fall of 2005 the annual field survey found "incredible numbers" of juvenile yellowtails. The survey biologist reported that the "numbers were astounding" (CFN February 2006:1B).

What could one surmise from this record of frequent and abrupt changes in stock sizes? It might be suspected from this record that yellowtails may naturally be subject to substantial variability, and that "stability" or "sustainability" or MSY are concepts that are not appropriate for the species. In fact, this kind of variability is a natural characteristic of some kinds of species of natural biological systems - ecosystems - and is to be expected and cannot be managed for stability. Yellowtails may be an example of that natural and relative instability of some components of the ecosystem that we noted earlier (p. 187) was suggested by The Task Force. An operational concept of ecosystems tells us how we may identify such species.

An operational hypothesis of ecosystems

It is helpful to focus on a particular hypothesis of the nature of ecosystems – *a hierarchical concept of ecosystems* – in order to understand the apparently large and possibly natural fluctuations of yellowtail flounder. The concept has many dimensions, so we will only summarize it here. A thorough exploration of the hierarchical concept of ecosystems is presented in O'Neill et al. (1986), in several works by T.F.H. Allen and his colleagues (e.g. Allen et al., 2003), and by Apollonio (2002) with a focus on fisheries. The hypothesis recognizes that hierarchical phenomena are universal in nature, from microscopic cells to the functioning of organs within organisms to the functions of ecosystems and of the biosphere as a whole. Such hierarchical characteristics are also common in our social and economic systems, such as in the military, the judiciary, or the Federal Reserve System. The hierarchy in all cases is basically that of constraints of various kinds upon rates of processes within the system of interest. That is to say, the components of systems have characteristic dynamics or rates of processes, and those rates of processes may be usefully perceived to be arranged in hierarchical levels. The rates of processes are generally slower at higher levels of hierarchies and those slower rates act as constraints upon faster processes at lower levels.

In a fish system the various species have characteristically different growth, birth, or death rates. Seldom would different species have the same rates. To reiterate here, the central idea at the heart of the hierarchical concept of ecosystems suggests that slower rates of a system constrain the faster rates of other components of the system. Thus, for example, in the sea the dynamics of zooplankton - birth rates, growth rates, reproductive rates, death rates - are much faster than those of krill-eating whales, but krill do not proliferate without limits because their numbers - their dynamics of reproduction and growth - are constrained at least in part by whales, which have much slower rates. There is thus a hierarchy of constraints upon rates of processes in the whale-krill system. This hierarchical arrangement of rates of processes - or functions - indicates that in general components with slow and relatively stable dynamics, such as whales, are found higher in the hierarchy, and components with faster and less stable dynamics, such as krill, are found lower in the hierarchy. The top of a hierarchy is defined by the slower, constraining dynamics of the system.

As a further example, codfish are a highly prolific fish, but in an unfished ocean system codfish do not fill the ocean in spite of their astonishing fecundity. The natural dynamics of cod and other species may be constrained not only by predation or disease but also by the somewhat technical concept of a *guild*. A guild (Root 1967) is a group of species, such as groundfish, that exploits the same environmental resources in a similar way in approximately the same place. The resource the guild uses may be food, or spawning grounds, or perhaps hiding places such as burrows on the edge of the continental shelf for tile fishes or lobsters. Thus the phenomenon of competition is part of this concept of guilds - competition for food or perhaps certain kinds of space. Because there is a finite resource to be exploited and the several species of a guild must compete for it, there is imposed upon any single species in the guild a limit to its numbers as constrained by the guild - by all the other species, or the community of species, competing for the same resource. The guild, collectively, has slower dynamics than any member species and therefore by definition occupies a higher level in an ecosystem hierarchy and sets a certain stability upon any of its member species by preventing unduly large variations in numbers.

The yellowtail example

What we know about yellowtail flounder dynamics suggests that it is relatively low in a hierarchical system of fishes, very roughly akin to krill with respect to whales. One way of estimating relative positions of species within hierarchies may be by comparing their life history characteristics. It is instructive to compare the characteristics of several species of flounders. [77]

	Depth (meters)	Size (pounds)	Maturity (years)	Egg numbers (thousands)	Egg sizes (mm)
Yellowtail	10-80	1-2	2-4	350-4,570	0.9
Winter flounder	50-90	3	3	500-3,300	0.8
Dab or plaice	40-200	1-6	3	500-2,200	2.5
Witch flounder	90-330	3-4	4.5	350	1-1.5
Halibut	up to 1,000	600	12	2,200	3-3.8

Compared in this way, there is clearly a systematic change in characteristics as flounders are found from shallow to deep waters. The changes reflect the hierarchical order we have in mind, and the changes reflect the relative stabilities of the environments in which those flounders live. The fishes with the fastest rates (earliest maturity, greatest fecundity) live in the least stable shallow waters, and halibuts live in the most stable deep waters. (The large egg numbers of halibut reflect their very large sizes - up to 700 pounds.)

Of all the flounder species, yellowtails are found in shallowest waters and because of that environment they may be subject to quite large temperature fluctuations such as abnormally warm summers or cold winters. All the yellowtail characteristics are typical or symptomatic of a variable, unstable species relatively low in the hierarchy of a fisheries ecosystems. Winter flounder, which also live mostly in shoal waters, have characteristics more similar to yellowtail than to dabs, which live in deeper waters. It is characteristic of animals in general that those that are inherently unstable have these characteristics; that is, they are, among other things, relatively small, mature at an early age, and produce a large number of small eggs. Animals that live in such variable

---

[77] Data from Collette and Klein-MacPhee 2002.

environments are generally recognized to have rather fast dynamics (e. g., birth and growth rates) that allow them to respond quickly to and recover from adverse conditions. Such species typically live in variable environments and their life history characteristics or dynamics are adaptations naturally selected for survival in those habitats. NMFS in fact reported that the "boom and bust" pattern of yellowtail fluctuations through four decades (1940s-1970s) was associated with temperature conditions, "with abundance declining sharply during warm temperature years" (CFN May 1983:24). Michael Sissenwine (1974), then a scientist at the Northeast Fisheries Science Center of NMFS, has shown that water temperature and year-class strength are correlated - cooler temperatures promoting larger year-classes.

We do not insist that a low position in the hierarchy and therefore inherent instability is in fact the case for yellowtail; we do say that it *may* be, and that if we better understood marine ecosystems we would be in a much stronger position to determine whether such is the case. We suggest that understanding the *normal* functions of marine systems could greatly simplify and improve the task of fisheries management. If in fact yellowtail is one of those species that naturally exhibit substantial variations in biomass, then great efforts to "stabilize" it or to maintain it at some particular, "sustainable" level of biomass is not a potentially profitable management exercise and would impose unnecessary costs on the industry and upon enforcement and management. The record in New England shows that in spite of many unreported catches, discards, and reported catches greatly in excess of quotas, yellowtail flounders *increased* markedly in numbers from 1978 to 1983. But then landings declined forty percent one year later in 1984. This decline was considered by NMFS to be the result of removal of quotas under the Interim Plan and the large increase in landings. But it could also reflect an inherently unstable nature of the species. The complex and costly management efforts that were directed to yellowtail without discernible benefit could be much more profitably spent on species within the system that do require special efforts for stock stabilizations. The hypothesis of how ecosystems are hierarchically structured tells us that such species requiring careful management are those, like halibut, that are high in the hierarchy. They are vulnerable to fishing effort and do not recover quickly, primarily because their dynamics are generally slow; they are slow to reach maturity, they often (not always) are of relatively low fecundities, they grow slowly to large sizes (and are therefore desirable in the market), and they may be a particular target for heavy fishing effort.

Species that are characteristically higher or lower in natural hierarchical systems are subject to different *kinds* of constraints (Steele 1980, Apollonio 2002:143). Those higher species are generally constrained by biological (or even social [78]) forces, while those lower species are typically constrained by inanimate physical forces. For example, by the same criteria used for flounders here, herring rank higher than mackerel. In the Gulf of St. Lawrence it was found that mackerel biomass in the first year of life is largely determined by temperature, but the growth of herring responds to the combined biomass of herring and mackerel (Mann 1982). We should expect, then, that yellowtail flounder, with the basic life-history parameters typical of species relatively low in a hierarchical system, would be constrained by physical forces - temperature - and would naturally vary substantially in numbers. The hierarchical concept therefore tells us what kinds of factors - whether physical or biological constraints - to consider for the management of particular species. It suggests how we may best focus our limited resources and where within the system to most profitably direct our management efforts.

Exploring the concept of hierarchy theory

There is another characteristic of hierarchical systems that is very relevant for fisheries management. The essence of the hierarchical

---

[78] There is reason to believe that young codfish off Newfoundland are "taught" essential migration routes by their elders (Rose 1993).

hypothesis is that the higher levels, those of slower dynamics, may constrain the dynamics of lower levels, such as whales constrain zooplankton dynamics. Such constraints tend to stabilize and lend predictability to systems and thereby make management of systems possible. The National Research Council (1999:115) at least implicitly recognized this phenomenon: "For example, the role that top predators play in stabilizing ecosystems has been studied extensively." The report went on to say that, "However incomplete our knowledge about ecosystems principles, what is known should be given formal consideration in fisheries-management decisions." We agree, and we suggest that the hierarchical concept of ecosystems tells us much of importance about ecosystems characteristics that should be considered for management. For example, it is common in fishing to preferentially target the larger, older, and slower-growing fish of a species (the traditional management tactic intended to achieve MSY advocates and endorses this practice) and the larger species of a system. The result is that that practice leaves smaller individuals of a species and smaller fish species. This is known as "fishing down the food web", a phenomenon that Pauley and MacLean (2003) have described for the entire North Atlantic and the world's oceans. If the larger, or higher, levels, with their constraints upon the system, are removed, then greater variabilities in the lower levels must be expected; the then unconstrained and more rapid dynamics of lower levels will lead to greater variability and instability and perhaps eventually to destabilization of the whole system. Pauly and MacLean (2003:56) summarize it this way:

> Fish species targeted by fisheries, earlier very predictable in terms of their biomasses, now fluctuate more widely than before.

> This effect, moreover, has been amplified by the scarcity of old specimens in the exploited populations, whose magnitude, therefore, tends to vary with reproductive success, i. e., the entry of young fish ("recruits") into the populations. Combined, these two effects make catches even harder to predict, and fisheries more difficult to

manage than they already were.

The removal of a governor - a constraint - on an engine (a mechanical system of parts with differing dynamics) has an analogous effect; the engine will race and sputter, race and sputter, and perhaps eventually burn itself out.

Earlier we expressed our doubt that forecasts of fish conditions could be made by finding predictive indices at the earliest life stages. We return to that question here. The presence of a governor is a constraint upon the dynamics of an engine; with the governor functioning properly the behavior or performance of an engine and its parts are reasonably predictable. And Pauly and MacLean (2003:56), whom we have just quoted, make essentially the same point: with the reduction of larger, older fishes (or larger, slower growing species) from a community, constraints upon the dynamics of community components are removed and catches become even harder to predict and management becomes more difficult. It is within the presence of constraints at higher hierarchical levels limiting the dynamics of species that fisheries predictions are possible. As the National Research Council noted, the presence of top predators lends stability to ecosystems - and stable systems are predictable. The lesson is that predictability is made possible by maintaining the higher levels of communities or systems.

The primary focus, then, of fisheries management should be directed to the top of the hierarchy, that is, to those components that exhibit the slower dynamics, because it is within them that stabilization of the whole system lies. This amounts to preservation of the "context" of the dynamics of components of the system - or to the preservation of a "governor" on the engine.

How fishing removes stabilizing constraints

Constraints may be removed not only among species within fisheries systems but also within a single species or a population. Many marine fish populations in their unexploited state consisted of a number of mature year classes. Herring no doubt typically had more than ten mature year classes prior to heavy exploitation. But fishing in some cases has reduced herring populations to five or even fewer year classes.

Fisheries typically target the largest individuals available in a population. The largest fish are usually the oldest, the (then) slowest growing, and the most difficult to replace of the population's members. As the largest individuals are fished out, attention turns to progressively smaller fish until - as in many groundfish fisheries - the size of exploitable fish is at or barely above the minimum legal size (Auster and Shackell 1997:160).

Such removals of older year classes are in fact the removal of constraints. The older year classes have slower dynamics than younger year classes and because of that may act as constraints upon the growth, feeding, or other dynamics of the younger fish. Older fishes of some species, particularly very fecund species such as codfish, are cannibalistic upon their young, thus constraining an overabundance of juveniles. It is not uncommon that as older fish are removed the variability and unpredictability of the remaining, younger, fish increase.

A related phenomenon is the decrease in age of maturity - of first reproduction - in organisms. Reproduction at young ages is typical of inherently unstable species; yellowtails mature earlier than the other flounders. Reproduction at an early age can be a normal characteristic of certain species whether exploited or not, but it can also be a result of heavy exploitation of species that normally reproduce at older ages. In either case the result is reduced stability and predictability of the species. In the 1920s the youngest mature haddock found off New England - only two out of 1300 fish examined - were about four years old (Bigelow and Schroeder 1953:204). Sinclair and Murawski (1997:78 Fig. 3.4) reported that the age (and size) of maturity of haddock on Georges Bank has declined: "In 1963, the youngest fish to mature were age 3. In 1969 more than one fourth of age-2 fish matured.

By 1987, even some age-1 fish were reproductively mature."
Sinclair and Murawski noted that the reduction of age of maturity
was more likely a consequence rather than a cause of the stock
decline. But there is a strong probability that earlier maturity
contributes to instability of stocks and such instabilities may lead
to ever increasing amplitudes of oscillations with an increasing
risk of stock collapse. Both the reduction of numbers of year
classes and the reduction of age and size at maturity are in fact
removals of constraints upon the dynamics of a species and
contributors to greater variabilities of a population.

We recall the statement to NEFMC in the fall of 1994 that the
spawning stock biomass of haddock had collapsed and that the
council was faced with a fifteen-to-twenty year problem. But only
two years later the spawning stocks of cod, haddock and
yellowtail on Georges Bank were increasing; the spawning stock
biomass of Georges Bank haddock approximately doubled
between 1994 and 1996. In 2002 extraordinary numbers of young
haddock appeared. We have noted the variations of cod from
1999 to 2001. These sorts of oscillations of numbers are
characteristic of destabilized populations of organisms. And it is
for this reason we may view with some concern the claim that the
great numbers - "an astonishing one billion haddock in a single
year" (*Portland Press Herald*, Feb. 7, 2004:2B) - of a single year
class of young haddock, the largest on record - in the fall of 2003
is an indication of the rebuilding of haddock stocks off New
England. [79] We hope that it is, but if the hierarchical concept of
ecosystems is correct, the haddock boom may reflect the great
oscillations and instabilities to be expected in a severely deranged
population. The boom in young haddock in 2003 may well
indicate not a stock recovery but one that may decline severely.
Recruitment of young haddock in the following year - 2004 - was
apparently among the smallest on record, only one percent of that
of 2003. The eminent population ecologist G.E. Hutchinson
(1948) was perhaps the first to carefully examine this

---

[79] It was reported in 2006 that those fish were not growing, that they
were much delayed in reaching minimum legal size, for reasons not
understood (CFN August 2006:13A).

phenomenon. He noted that increasing oscillations without constraints inevitably lead to population crashes. It is for this reason that Robert O'Neill and his colleagues, who have thoroughly explored this concept, stated (O'Neill et al. 1986:211) that "the ecosystem shows instability whenever the constraints system is broken down.... Environmental managers must be careful never to introduce a perturbation that will disturb the system's natural constraints system." Unfortunately, the concept of maximum sustainable yield (MSY) is such a perturbation.

MSY removes constraints

MSY advocates that fishing should be carried out in such a way that large, old, slow-growing fishes are removed from a population of interest, leaving a preponderance of young, fast-growing fish. MSY proposes that the population will thereby attain its greatest natural rate of increase, which could thereby provide the maximum sustainable harvest. Such an attenuated population would indeed achieve its largest growth rate, but it is not sustainable. The application of the concept of MSY, in fact, removes the constraints of older fish in the population upon the dynamics of younger fish. That, indeed, is the explicit goal of MSY. But the younger fish may then begin those oscillations against which Hutchinson first and then O'Neill and his colleagues warned. MSY in effect shifts the characteristics of a population to a lower hierarchical level with inherently faster dynamics and greater instability and unpredictability. We should keep in mind the significance and consequences of multiple year classes in populations. They lend stability to populations and thus increase their chances of survival by reducing their natural variabilities, which can lead to extinction upon severe depletion. It is for this reason, among others, that there is natural selection pressure for species with longer lives, delayed maturity, and multiple year classes. The reduction of multiple year classes by efforts to attain MSY in fact works against the evolutionary adaptation of species to their environments.

One of the consequences of increased instabilities in species is that the costs of species assessments and management increase markedly. Rothschild, Sharov, and Lambert (1997:142) noted that "Single-species management relies heavily on mathematical models that require *current* biological data such as fish age, length, weight, and maturity" (emphasis added). (This would be equally true, or more so, of multispecies management.) But in species or populations from which constraints upon dynamics have been removed and then exhibit oscillations of increasing amplitudes in numbers, those parameters essential for the models will change significantly. Thus the challenge of acquiring *current* data becomes an ever-larger problem.

Simplifying management

A lesson learned from applying the hierarchical concept of ecosystems is that it is simpler, more feasible, and more effective to manage the higher components with slower dynamics than it is to attempt to individually manage the intrinsically variable components at lower levels of the system. Thus this concept of ecosystems tells us *where* to direct our primary management efforts; that is to say, how to use our limited management resources most effectively. And because it is easier to manage at higher levels than at lower levels, the management process should become simpler, cheaper, and more enforceable. It is for this reason that we view with concern the notorious Amendment 13 implemented in 2003. It is symptomatic of the ever-increasing complicatedness of fisheries management. The amendment consists of more than *1600* pages. (By contrast, in 1995 groundfish regulations filled forty-six pages of the Code of Federal Regulations.) Not all those pages are regulations, of course, but all 1600 pages, presumably, are required by MFCMA as it is now written, or at least by the administrative interpreta-tions of the requirements of MFCMA and other administrative acts and executive orders, or by a perceived necessity to defend the plan under possible (probable?) litigation in court. Here we may recall the prophetic words of the Development Sciences report (MS 1977:c) prepared in early 1977: "The council must function within a paperwork nightmare. FMPs require at the very least exhaustive descriptive material."

Symptomatic of this dilemma, also, is a common perception concerning multispecies management or of vaguely defined "ecosystems-based fisheries management." The perception is that it must encompass a very wide range of issues:

> Ideally, an ecosystem-based approach will allow for simultaneous consideration of risks to target species, prey species, by-catch species, protected species, essential fish habitat, secondary effects of fishing vessels and gear, and effects on fishing communities (Brodziak et al. 2004:539).

(This would seem to be an echo of the advice to the council in 1976 that it must separately manage fifty-six species.) And these authors went on to say:

> The costs of obtaining adequate data for assessment of all marine species actually or potentially affected by fisheries would probably be *exorbitant*, probably requiring at least a 10-fold increase in current monitoring levels, with concomitant increases in scientists and technicians to collect, process, manage, and analyze the data and communicate the results (emphasis added) (Brodziak et al. 200:541).

Hilborn, Punt, and Orensanz (1997:151) had previously observed that "Acquiring and managing data are very expensive, and full implementation of multispecies models - as they are presently conceived - remains problematical." They characterized the problems of such multispecies management as "formidable." And Peter Larkin (1996:150) cautioned that "Efforts of this kind, which seek verisimilitude with nature, are encumbered with a large number of parameters for which values cannot be gauged either precisely or independently."

This reality suggests that management has gone astray. It becomes ever more complex, burdensome, expensive, and confusing, with an increasing probability of decreasing efficacy. This trend is contrary to the principle of ecosystems functions that management would be more effective and *simplified* if applied at the proper hierarchical levels wherein lie the relevant constraints upon the components of interest within the system. It is for this reason we have reservations about the observation of the National Research Council report (1999:13) that "by *ecosystem-based management* of fisheries, this committee means an approach that seriously takes all major ecosystem components and services - both structural and functional - into account in managing fisheries." Howard Pattee (1973), a pioneering advocate of the hierarchical concept, summarized the principle of relative simplicity at higher levels succinctly: "The dynamics of control is determined by... how details are ignored." But we can agree with the second half of the NRC statement, as will become apparent later, that we should be "committed to understanding *larger ecosystems processes* for the goal of achieving sustainability in fishery management" (emphasis added). An agreement upon what we mean by "larger processes" will become critical.

Commenting on the quick-sand trap of including many parameters in vague concepts of ecosystems-based management, Allen, Tainter, and Hoekstra, proponents of the hierarchical concept, wrote (2003:48) that they

...do not recommend a slovenly holism that tosses everything into consideration all at once. Not only is the adage that everything is connected to everything else untrue (most terms in an interaction matrix are most sensibly set to zero), but surrendering to such a notion is intellectually paralyzing. If everything is indeed importantly connected to everything else at every scale according to every criterion, then there are no workable simplifying assumptions. Vague hand-waving about the whole system would indicate that there is nothing that can be done, and so it would follow that we should stop worrying about sustainability and brace ourselves for the collapse.

For this reason we find little comfort or guidance for ecosystems management in the definition of ecosystems offered by the National Research Council (1999:36): "Ecosystems are complex, linked, interactive systems in which organisms, habitats, and external forces (e.g., ocean currents, weather) act together to shape communities and regulate population abundances." Or (NRC 1999:105): "Ecological systems are complex interconnected nonlinear systems." Such definitions give little direction and convey a sense of complicatedness. They do not suggest a working, operational hypothesis for practical application to ecosystems-based fisheries management.

We repeat that the great appeal of the hierarchical concept of ecosystems is that it is a refutable, operational hypothesis that offers a much *simpler* strategy for fisheries management. That this is so is explained, in summary, by

> Howard Pattee's (1972) term *self-simplification*. He noted that complex systems, like organisms, possess upper-level structure that simplifies the behavior of the material of which they are made by imposing a small set of limits [i. e., constraints]....self-simplification improves predictability. All management depends on adequate predictions of the effect of management action, so predictability is critical for success. Complex systems are manageable, whereas equivalent complicated systems are not. For example, an organism can be managed, whereas an equivalent mass of chemical material cannot (Allen, Tainter, and Hoekstra 2003:421).

Complex systems in Pattee's sense are organized - self-simplified - in such a way as to bring order and predictability out of complicated or chaotic situations or collections of components. Pattee's principle of self-simplification is familiar to us all; it is essential for our individual well being. Our bodies are systems composed of many parts (structures) and functions (processes) all with differing dynamics. The many parts and processes are integrated by a hierarchical arrangement of constraints into the whole person. We as individuals would have time for nothing else if we had to consciously monitor and make adjustments for the proper functioning of heart, liver, lungs, kidneys, nervous system, muscle coordination, pituitary gland, ionic balance, carbon dioxide levels, blood chemistry.... But we don't have to because all those subcomponents and processes are integrated and constrained by the structure and physiology of the whole system. We can generally manage that immensely complex system and keep everything in balance and in good working order quite simply by a proper diet and exercise. Pattee's principle of self-simplification applies equally to human and fisheries systems. The difference between the human system and a fishery system is one of degree, not of kind.

Biological systems, whether organisms or ecosystems, evolve through development of hierarchical constraints toward order and predictability by the mechanisms of natural selection. Such order and predictability simplify the manageability of those systems.

Defining objectives and identifying systems

Earlier we made the point that clearly defined objectives are important in the context of ecosystems-based management of fisheries. The reason is that the "top" of the hierarchy depends upon the objective. The hierarchy may be altered or inverted without contradiction if the objectives change. Valerie Ahl and Timothy Allen (1996:98) explained this potentially confusing idea as follows:

> The ordering of levels in an empirical hierarchy depends on which aspect of the situation the observer considers significant. Change the significance, and the order of levels change. A pair of levels populated by their respective classes of entities could switch orders without there being any contradiction, if the question used to construct the hierarchy changes. If the question is, "Which species controls the number of the other as a food supply?" then the deer are the upper-level context of the wolf. Conversely, if the question is, "Which species controls the other through

predation" then the wolf is the upper contextual level for
the deer. The change from deer to wolf as the upper level
comes from changing the point of view. That change
identifies a different type of relationship between the two
animals.

This issue (wrote Apollonio 2002:148-9) is important to
fisheries management; it warrants some further
consideration. Suppose our objective for the lobster fishery
was optimization of catch or net income per fisherman. We
would then most likely implement a limited-entry and trap-
limit program. The right numbers of fishermen and traps
per fisherman could attain the objective. But suppose
instead our objective was to provide a possibility for
employment income for as many people as possible, in a
region where other economic opportunities were few,
accepting the fact that some would do better than others.
Here we would not be concerned with the size of any
particular income, only that there be opportunities for
income. In this case we would be concerned only with the
total number of lobsters that could be caught without
jeopardizing the well being of the resource. The two cases
would have different constraints, the first being an
economic constraint - that is, the ratio of the cost of harvest
compared to the value of the catch not to exceed a certain
value. The second case would have a biological constraint,
the size of the acceptable catch. Here again we see the
possibility of an inversion of hierarchical order.

We might try to apply this idea to the groundfish situation
confronting NEFMC. Is the objective to maximize the economic
efficiency of the harvesting of the resource? This was the explicit
intent of the Stratton Commission of 1969, which advocated the
smallest number of economically efficient vessels. Or is the
objective to preserve the traditional, diverse, and flexible fishing
industry of New England? The latter objective may not be very
"efficient" in a conventional economic sense, but it does provide
for a broad variety of employment opportunities in a region where

such opportunities vary widely in availability. Proponents of the first objective might consider ITQs as a strategy for attaining that objective. The proponents of the second objective would certainly avoid such schemes as ITQs, but would have to be concerned about total removals of fish from the stocks. These two possible objectives resemble those suggested above for the lobster fishery, and the two objectives are characterized by different dynamics and therefore entail different constraints, economic and biological, just as suggested for the lobster fishery.

Defining sustainability

We argue here for an ecosystems approach to fisheries management, but we have heard it said that fisheries do not need ecosystems management but management for sustainability. We agree, of course, with the importance of sustainable fisheries, but our argument is that sustainability is best attained by preserving those structures and functions - the natural constraints - of ecosystems that are essential if there is to be hope for sustainable fisheries. Sustainability has been defined "as maintaining, or fostering the development of, the system *contexts* that produce the goods, services, and amenities that people need or value, at an acceptable cost, for as long as they are needed or valued" (emphasis added) (Allen, Tainter, and Hoekstra (2003:26). If the systems contexts are not preserved, then sustainability is not possible, except perhaps with costly subsidies to systems.

Ecosystems have outputs, or products, and it is those outputs we wish to preserve and sustain by protecting or restoring ecosystems. The outputs consist of lumber, for example, or fish protein, or oxygen in the atmosphere, or temperature stabilizations, or water purification. Well-developed and healthy ecosystems produce these outputs, or we may say that they function, very well without help. We can say they do their jobs without subsidies. But as ecosystems are disrupted or attenuated, their outputs decline. Polluted wetlands can no longer be the nursery habitat of juvenile fish. Clear-cut tropical forests cannot control soil erosion that thus may threaten villages and indigenous agriculture. The National Research Council (1999:15, quoting from Kurien 1998) cites a traditional Asian coastal proverb that summarizes our concept of context very well: "Where there is water there is fish; if we take care of the water, the fish will take care of us."

Subsidizing stressed ecosystems

When society recognizes the consequences of a disrupted ecosystem, it may attempt remedial action to correct the damage done - often at great cost, whether successful or not. This is called *subsidization* of ecosystems. Thus we have flood-control projects, or erosion control projects, or water purification systems, or wetlands remediation. Society provides a subsidy to keep the ecosystem functioning to produce the products that society values. Fisheries management provides an example. Much effort and millions of dollars are spent annually producing hatchery fish to subsidize the loss of naturally spawned fish in rivers, for example, that have been degraded by siltation, pollution, dams, or overfishing. Great attempts were made by hatcheries in the past to subsidize lobster production in New England, and even now (2007) there is a new effort in eastern Maine to operate a hatchery to produce 100-150,000 young lobsters per year. There is currently considerable interest and activity in Maine and Canada to create hatcheries for groundfish, and as of this writing there is scheduled a two-day scallop enhancement (i. e., subsidy) workshop in Maine. The initial federal government role in fisheries management was to create the U.S. Fish Commission, that recommended fish hatcheries to alleviate the perceived decline of groundfish in the late nineteenth century. All of these are subsidies, at considerable cost to society, to ecosystems whose functions have been disrupted. The costs of subsidies are in proportion to the degree of systems derangement.

There is another dimension to the nature of subsidies. That is the proliferation of the administrative or bureaucratic apparatus involved in fisheries management. Fisheries management prior to heavy exploitation was a simple matter - in fact hardly noticeable at all. In New England in the 1930s and 1940s there was talk of a minimum mesh size for groundfish, and there were a few laws for recreational fish and shellfish. But with the ever-increasing exploitation of many species, management has become all-pervasive, multi-dimensional, expensive, confusing, and to date of tentative effectiveness.

> Whether successful or not, as presently operating fisheries management is very costly, and must be viewed as a form of subsidy to the industry, to the extent that management is viewed as enabling the orderly and maximum exploitation of fisheries resources.... [But] Management entails a large infrastructure of research, administration, monitoring, and regulatory entities, which are usually paid for by the taxpayers....not only have most management measures proved unable to control the rapid decline of almost all major commercial fisheries [around the North Atlantic], they have done so at great cost (Pauly and MacLean 2003:76).

Consider the lobster fishery. When the Maine fishery landed on average about 20 million pounds a year, there were essentially three laws - minimum and maximum sizes, no possession of egg-bearing females, and no-scrubbing of egg-carrying females. These laws were enforced more or less by the state fisheries agency. Now with Maine landings in excess of 60 million pounds per year, there remains the state agency with a good many more laws, and there is also a regional management plan administered by the Atlantic States Marine Fisheries Commission that in turn is supervised by NMFS. The regional ASMFC plan consists of several management zones, each with a committee of advisors and scientists. The State of Maine, in addition, has seven lobster management zones each attended by a council of harvesters, and each zone is given administrative support by the state agency. By all reports, the meetings of the zone councils are time-consuming and contentious. There are also, incidentally, two zone councils for Maine's collapsed sea urchin fishery.

As the problems of fisheries management have continued with, at best, modest progress, the underlying structure of the management process has come under increasing scrutiny. One suggestion given considerable attention is that there should be multi-layered management structures; that is, general oversight in the national interest, regional management as with the existing regional councils, and subregional and local councils that presumably would be better informed and better positioned to respond to the local realities of fish stocks. There are, in addition to this proposed formal hierarchical structure, proposals for much greater involvement by "stakeholders" in the management process at the several levels. This way of thinking is captured in the phrase "match complexity with complexity." That is, because the fisheries are perceived to be complex, the management apparatus must be equally complex. The National Research Council (1999:9) apparently endorsed this point of view: "the spatial and temporal scales at which the institutional structures operate should better match those of important processes that affect fisheries." And further (NRC 1999:92): "A major challenge is developing institutional structures with sufficient complexity in scope and scale to be appropriate for complex and dynamic ecological systems." This of course ignores Howard Pattee's principle of self-simplification, and no one to our knowledge has calculated the costs - money and time and effort by participants - of this multi-layered proposal, but undoubtedly they would be large. Indeed, it has been 'guesstimated' that for the world as a whole, the present cost of fisheries subsidies and management may equal or exceed the net value of the fisheries.

One may consider all of these existing and proposed costs to be a subsidy to the ecosystem, and since they are substantial we may conclude that they are an indication of an ecosystem that is seriously deranged.

The hierarchical concept of ecosystems in the sense of O'Neill and his colleagues (1986) and of Allen, Tainter, and Hoekstra (2003) develops the argument that properly managed ecosystems do not require artificial subsidies to continue to produce their goods and services, and that only in that condition is the production of those goods and services truly sustainable. Sustainable fisheries therefore are dependent upon, and are a consequence of, informed ecosystems management which preserves the *context* of the system in which the outputs - the fish - are produced.

Management based on a hierarchical concept of ecosystems

We suggest here an example of a management plan that incorporates the principles of the hierarchical concept of ecosystems. It offers an *operational* hypothesis for the practical application of a concept of ecosystems and thereby may remove much of the present vague or ill-defined ideas of ecosystems that impede the application of the concept to fisheries management.

As an introduction to this example of a management plan, we repeat here for emphasis and clarification the essentials of the hierarchical concept of ecosystems:

1) Many natural and social/economic/judicial/military systems exhibit analogous hierarchical structures and functions.

2) The hierarchy in all cases is that of a series of constraints of various kinds upon rates of processes in the systems.

3) Slower rates of processes are found at the higher levels; faster rates of processes are found at the lower levels. The slower rates define the "top" of the hierarchy; the faster rates define the "bottom."

4) Faster rates of processes at lower levels in the hierarchy are constrained by slower rates of processes at the higher levels. The higher level of slower rates, or dynamics, is the *context* within which the level of particular interest (e.g., codfish) functions.

5) Effective management of a system depends upon (a)

preservation of the hierarchical structure and functions - the context, and (b) identification of the appropriate level of constraint for the hierarchical level of particular interest. The level of interest is most effectively managed at a higher level of constraint upon the lower level of interest. The hierarchical concept tells us that it is the *context* of - the constraints upon - the level of interest, not the level of interest itself, that should be managed. The constraints tend to stabilize systems and lend predictability to them. If the context is preserved (or managed) such that it retains its natural, inherent, stabilizing constraints, then the individual subcomponents at lower levels of systems may be left to look after themselves. The hierarchical concept tells us that we should manage to preserve the context and not the subcomponents (the products; e.g., codfish) of systems (Allen, Tainter, and Hoeksta 2003).

> We have noted... that environmental management becomes ineffective when we manage for the outputs of productive systems rather than for the systems themselves....Such production systems experience endless variations in output, so managing for their outputs entails attending to myriad details. This approach was described as like sticking one's finger in the dike (Allen, Tainter, and Hoekstra 2003:385).

(It seems to us that this describes exactly the situation the council experienced in April 2002 when it was informed that the scientific advice upon which it had based Amendment 9 no longer was valid and that it must therefore undertake a new amendment to the groundfish plan - stick its finger once more into another hole in the dike.)

6) Management at the appropriate higher level of context and constraint is simpler, cheaper, and more effective than attempts to directly manage the lower levels of particular interest.

The Federal Reserve analogy

A familiar example of the hierarchical concept of systems

structure and function is the Federal Reserve System. The FED conforms in every way to the hierarchical concept of ecosystems.

The FED manages the myriad activities of a very diverse and complicated economy by a fundamentally very simple and generally effective method. It adjusts interest rates, as it sees fit for the greatest overall benefit to the nation, to stimulate or constrain business activity. It makes no attempt to manipulate the individual businesses of the nation or even segments of them. Such an undertaking would be counterproductive, in fact impossible. If attempted, it would create turmoil and chaos. Instead, the FED preserves freedom of choice for investors and businesses. They must be able to respond to unanticipated and unpredictable variables as they see fit. The FED leaves it to individual investors and businesses to make their own financial decisions, only within the constraints of interest rates.

A fisheries management proposal

As an example of the hierarchical concept applied to fisheries management we offer a specific proposal. But it is only one example from a number of possibilities that could be based on the hierarchical concept. Our proposal for fisheries management adopts a model very similar to that of the FED, for very similar reasons. Fisheries have a number of similarities to the nation's economy. They are not monolithic. They are diverse and complicated, and with many not-well-understood interactions. It is this reality that is in part responsible for the present complicated, confusing, costly, and perhaps unproductive attempts at individual species fisheries management.

Our proposal has the purpose of attaining a viable fishing industry. This goal depends upon 1) robust stocks of fish and 2) sustainable economics. Without these two elements in reasonable balance with each other there can be no viable fishing industry. Optimum yield, as required and defined by law, is attained when these two elements are in balance, or in proper relation to each other. Thus both biology and economics are equally incorporated in this purpose of management and in our proposed model for implementation. Viable fisheries would in this sense provide the greatest overall benefit to the nation.

The context of the fishing industry as a whole is economics. And many of the stabilizing constraints upon individual species are found within the aggregate of the species - within the community of species. It is the community of species that provides the context for the individual species; the natural constraints upon individual species are found within the integrity of the biological community structure. For this reason the community structure must be preserved if the natural stabilizing constraints to be found in community structure upon various species are to be preserved. The community structure may be preserved by *moderate* fishing across a *wide spectrum* of species.

The hierarchy with which we are concerned in this proposal, then, is:

Economics constrains the fishing industry, which constrains the natural community that constrains individual species. Both economics and the fish *community* must be equally incorporated in this proposal.

Our proposal does not attempt to directly manipulate the stock size of any single species. The hierarchical concept tells us that it is more effective to preserve the context in which individual species may vary within natural limits set by the constraints of the context.

Our model, therefore, proposes to monitor the collective *rate* of investment in the fisheries – *all* of the fisheries of the region - and the *rate* of biomass removals from the fish community of the region. It is *rates* that are of primary interest, not absolute numbers. As the rates of investment and removal vary, so would the third component of the model vary - the rate of a *conservation assessment* added to the cost of fuel of *all* fishing vessels. The conservation assessment is analogous to interest rates set by the FED. It would have the same purpose as interest rates set by the

FED.

As the rate of investment and/or of removals increased, so would the conservation assessment increase at an exponential rate sufficient to discourage additional investment or removals. As they declined, so would the assessment.

In short, the proposal states that the conservation assessment is a function of the rate of investment and the rate of removal. If one or the other or both go up or down, then the assessment changes accordingly.

Our proposal provides for and encourages diversifying both fishing effort and landings, and it discourages excessive fishing of any single species. It does this by "weighting" the contributions of individual species landings to the total aggregate landings according to their relative biomasses. Scarce Gulf of Maine cod would be weighted heavily; plentiful red hakes would be lightly weighted. This weighting could be done infrequently, perhaps biennially. A further refinement would be to weight the species according to their relative positions within the community-systems hierarchy: that is, species relatively low in the hierarchy, such as mackerel or perhaps yellowtail flounder, would be lightly weighted because of their inherent natural variability and their innate ability to recover rather quickly from depletion. Species higher in the hierarchy, such as halibut or redfish, would be more heavily weighted because, as a result of their slower dynamics, they are particularly vulnerable to depletions and do not rapidly recover. Further, species higher in the hierarchy should be more heavily weighted because they do provide constraints to lower components of the community and thereby lend stability to the entire community. This kind of weighting, because it is based on innate characteristics of species need be done only once. The biological argument for this kind of weighting is presented in Apollonio (2002). The formula for conservation assessment rates could be adjusted, perhaps annually, with experience to accomplish the desired level of incentives or disincentives for investments and removals.

The rates of investment would be estimated from IRS records of the fishing industry in aggregate. The rates of biomass removals would be estimated from landings records and the usual scientific stock assessments. No doubt there are techniques for estimating optimal relationships among the three components - investments, removals, and assessments - to achieve the desired balance between investments and removals. Continual or frequent adjustments of the conservation assessment would not be necessary. It may be that annual or possibly biennial adjustments would be sufficient.

Possible benefits

There are numerous advantages in this model compared to the present management system.

1) It preserves and restores individual choice among fishermen for all of their investment and fishing decisions, as they have always adapted to changing fishing conditions.

2) It encourages diversity of landings by species and preserves traditional flexibility to shift among species and fisheries. It encourages fishing on stocks in good condition and discourages fishing on stressed stocks.

3) It minimizes costly enforcement at sea except perhaps for some significant closed spawning areas. (Minimum fish sizes and mesh sizes would be retained. There is a disincentive - the heavily weighted stressed species in the model - to use small meshes for large-mesh species.)

4) It provides an incentive for *all* fishermen, collectively, to restrain or reduce capacity and effort - for all of our fisheries are overcapitalized.

5) It eliminates the constant necessity of continual species-by-species adjustments in trip limits, days-at-sea, closed areas etc.,

and the costly, time-consuming, and often-unproductive necessity for fishermen to attend frequent management meetings.

6) It eliminates incentives for high-grading, discards, and other wasteful practices.

7) Bycatches could be legally landed - and counted.

8) It provides an index by which potential investors and lending institutions may anticipate future conditions and judge the wisdom of new investments.

9) It removes the necessity or reasons for limited entry, ITQs, and other restrictive, socially manipulative schemes.

10) It eliminates the need for costly, uncertain, and unending efforts at estimating fishing effort at sea and similar parameters in the present management system.

11) It offers the option of achieving Optimum Yield, in fact, by adjusting the balance between the investment and the removal components of the model.

This proposal could meet all of the specific subobjectives identified by NEFMC in July 1978 as part of its ADF plan.

There may be concern that this proposal apparently does not attempt to *directly* limit the depletion by fishermen of particular species or stocks of the fisheries system. It may be suggested that in complex systems there must be a control mechanism for each component, otherwise the whole thing must fly apart. This may well be true for *engineered systems*, but such systems are an imperfect analogy for complex biological systems. Engineered systems are *deterministic* in the sense considered earlier. Such determinism mandates control mechanisms. Biological systems are not deterministic, but are suffused with indeterminacies, as Karl Popper pointed out, which is to say that some components of ecological systems naturally exhibit considerable variabilities of a relatively unpredictable kind. Nevertheless, the system as a whole does not fly apart, but is naturally resilient to and normally accommodates such uncertainties among its components.

Even so, our proposal here does not eschew *constraints* upon components of the system other than a *conservation* assessment added to fuels. Rather, by its intended purpose of achieving *moderate* fishing pressure upon a *diversity* of species, it seeks to preserve the *context* - the community structure and functions - of the system within which the natural constraints are found. Those natural constraints inherent in intact ecosystems are roughly analogous to the control mechanisms of engineered systems. But constraints evolved by the process of natural selection over the eons must be much more robust and effective than the demonstrably weak constraints of traditional management strategies. We, from our experience, are skeptical of attempts to artificially construct specific fisheries control mechanisms for all components of multispecies fisheries systems. Such attempts, history tells us, are expensive, stimulate noncompliance, and have unanticipated and usually undesirable consequences. And they are rather feeble and less likely to be effective in stabilizing natural systems than naturally evolved stabilizing constraints.

There are of course some species that are particularly vulnerable to overfishing. But by "weighting" the landings of vulnerable species, our proposal would discourage fishing pressure on those species. And what of those fishermen who nevertheless might chose to "hammer" such species? Two factors might soon dissuade them: peer pressure arising from the near certainty of rising conservation assessments added to fuel prices for all fishermen, and rapidly diminishing landings receipts, i. e., income, from those species.

This proposal closely follows the only operational hypothesis - the hierarchical concept of ecosystems - for ecosystems-based management of fisheries. It offers a familiar model, based upon our experience with the FED. It would be much simpler, more effective, and far less costly than the present management efforts.

We offer this proposal as an example of a management plan based on the hierarchical concept. It is simply one of a number of possible plans. The hierarchical concept of systems applies to a wide variety of natural and human-devised systems - to galactic, economic, physiological, military, academic, and judicial systems as well as ecosystems - and so it is adaptable to and appropriate for many practical applications (Ahl and Allen 1996). It holds the promise and potential for a variety of models that may be designed for particular fisheries situations and management objectives as managers see fit.

Initiation of a hierarchical concept of management

How would NEFMC, or any management authority, adopt and implement such a management strategy as we propose? The first step is to understand - thoroughly understand - and adopt an explicit operational hypothesis of what an ecosystem is, because vague hand-waving about the whole array of components in the sea will not help much. An explicitly defined hypothesis would provide a firm foundation and direction for a management strategy. If the hierarchical concept we advocate here were adopted, once the concept is *fully* understood and agreed upon, the management authority must then clarify its management objectives, because, as we have tried to make clear, the council's objectives or purposes would have much to do with the hierarchical ordering of constraints relevant to the levels of interest. At this time, whether deliberately or inadvertently, the purpose of NEFMC is to achieve scientifically determined BRPs, strictly numerical measures of stock sizes or fishing rates. This of course is only tenuously related to the congressional intent of Optimum Yield. There are other possible and equally legitimate management objectives. Perhaps the council would choose to encourage maximum economic efficiency in the catching of fish, or perhaps it would choose to encourage a fishery that would sustain small and dispersed communities that have few other employment opportunities. Or perhaps it would hope to perpetuate the New England tradition of family-owned fishing vessels. These are quite different possible objectives - there are others; Link (2002) lists seven, and the important determining dynamics would be different for each. The council would then focus on the dynamics of that hierarchical level that constrains the dynamics of the levels or objective of particular concern; the council would focus on preserving the context for the dynamics of the objective. A purpose, and the dynamics, that encouraged small diverse fishing communities, for example, would be significantly different from that which sought to achieve maximum economic efficiency in the fisheries. The constraints relevant to the latter purpose lie within vertically integrated corporate structures. An objective that sought to retain and encourage small, diverse fishing communities would have to insure equal access of all fishermen to a diversity of species - a goal and a strategy quite different from that of enhancing conventional economic efficiency. How, in fact, the council would plan to implement one or the other of these contrasting purposes would depend upon those dynamics that either encourage corporate operations or ownership of the fisheries, such as creation of ITQs, or that encourage a moderate rate of fishing over a wide diversity of species and preserves the flexibility of individual fishermen to make their own decisions based upon the prevailing local conditions. We believe we have suggested the outline of such a system with our proposal that is analogous to the practices of the Federal Reserve System.

As we have tried to emphasize previously, the job of identifying a fisheries management plan's purposes or objectives or function in potentially useful and productive terms is difficult but essential for hope of success. This is particularly true if the plan were to be based upon the hierarchical concept of ecosystems - apparently the only operational hypothesis of ecosystems principles - because the relevant hierarchy is determined by the agreed-upon objectives.

12) Conclusions

NEFMC has had, for over thirty years, a stormy, contentious, agonizingly difficult career, increasingly subjected to litigation and to ever-increasingly stringent rules under which it must operate. MFCMA is indeed an experiment in natural resources management, and the part-time members of the councils created by MFCMA in 1976 were catapulted into a learning and testing experience the magnitude and difficulty of which no one could have anticipated. The experiment, the learning, the difficulties continue; given the biological, economic, and sociological complexities and uncertainties of fisheries perhaps they always will.

Even so, NEFMC can state that a number of stocks under its jurisdiction in recent years have increased in numbers, not in three to seven years as NMFS forecast in 1976 but rather in twenty years and more. Critics may claim that the long period of partial and tentative recovery is attributable to lack of commitment, for whatever reason, to "tough" management by the council. We suspect the delay is more likely a necessary consequence of the lack of experience by all participants - scientists and managers - in practical management of complex fisheries, lack of efficacious tactics, and problems inherent in mixed-species groundfisheries.

Whether the partial recoveries are the result of effective, albeit delayed, management or good luck is debatable. If by effective management, that is, because of the ever-increasing restrictions put on the industry by Amendment 5 and its successors, there arises a key question for the future of the fisheries. Suppose the stocks are fully restored to levels defined by biological reference points, how then are they to be *sustained* at those levels?

Assuming that drastic measures, as in fact have been applied to the fisheries, were necessary to rebuild fish stocks from very low levels of the mid-1970s and the 1990s, are those same drastic measures to continue indefinitely into the future? The present moratorium on new permits is, according to the council plan, for the "rebuilding period." What happens when the stocks are rebuilt?

We have identified a number of serious problems inherent in the effort-control tactics that have been applied to date - problems not just for the industry, but problems also because of their impacts upon the resources themselves. Will management knowingly continue with such regulations that entail great costs to fishing communities, management agencies, fisheries scientists, enforcement authorities, and to fish populations and communities? Or will management begin to look for alternatives with which we may have some confidence that fish stocks in fact will be managed for sustainability at a reasonable cost to all interested entities and in conformity with the mandated National Standards? We suspect that if the current tactics are continued and applied to the industry if and when stocks are restored, then the existing problems and costs burdening the council, the federal government, and the industry can only continue.

Fisheries resources are public property and the public is entitled to an accounting for the full costs of managing the resources - the costs of assessments at sea and in research facilities for estimating the status of stocks, the costs of plan preparations and administrations, the costs of enforcement, the costs of litigation, and the costs to fishing communities which must adjust to regulations. We anticipate that the public in time will come to ask whether the benefits are commensurate with the costs.

We have reviewed a long list of real problems with which the council has struggled. They fall into two general categories: 1) "administrative" issues such as a long and obscure plan review process, tensions between NEFMC and the federal government concerning the locus of management authority, uncertainties in the process of regulation implementations, and the lack of definition or agreement on critical terms or concepts underlying the management objectives and process; and 2) fundamental problems created by the imperfect selectivity and other characteristics of the existing fishing technology, the very questionable efficacy of traditional strategies for effort control, and the inherently imprecise nature of traditional scientific advice and the near absence of an understanding or a working hypothesis of the structures and functions or dynamics of marine fisheries systems.

The problems in the first category could be resolved by political action, by congressional clarification of its intent with respect to MFCMA itself, or perhaps by a different structure of the management bodies. It could be argued that the problems of the first category are integral to the fishery council structure and could only be solved by abolishing MFCMA and the eight regional councils, as an original congressional sponsor of MFCMA considered to be an option, and by setting up a new management structure. There are those who argue that the Sustainable Fisheries Act of 1996, which amended MFCMA, should be repealed because it mandates rigid and unrealistic conditions upon management plans for fisheries that are inherently variable and subject to influences not fully understood, predictable, or controllable.

It is very probably politically unrealistic to suppose that MFCMA or its amendments could be or would be abolished in the foreseeable future, but its administrative or bureaucratic limitations or deficiencies ought to be acknowledged, and it would be a useful exercise to think about a model management structure that might replace it. As an example, we have summarized the ASMFC northern shrimp management process in its early days. The nine-member ASMFC shrimp management board (three members from each of three states) in its annual one-day meeting received scientific advice and recommendations from industry, and on that day made its decisions for the following year. Its decisions were not subject to higher review; it had full authority to use its best judgment. Its decisions were final. The industry left the one-day meeting knowing the rules for the following year; it could make its business plans accordingly. Granted the northern shrimp fishery is a much simpler fishery than the New England groundfish fishery, but the complexities and uncertainties of the multispecies fishery are in themselves an argument for the management body of whatever form, knowledgeable and experienced in the fishery, to have full and final authority to use its best judgment, to make decisions in a timely manner, and to have the opportunity to learn from and correct its mistakes as necessary and in a timely manner.

The present system suffers from the multiple burdens of great complexity, great uncertainty in its rule-making authority, arbitrary deadlines, and no clear point of final responsibility. In theory the councils make the rules, but in practice NOAA/NMFS determines the rules, or increasingly it may be the court. Or it may be that the court, having made a ruling, reverses itself and mandates a management option it had previously rejected. It is a fact that regulations for which the industry had made plans have been changed before they came into effect or before results, good or bad, could be expected from them - as happened with Amendment 9.

Within the fishing industry, there is continuing, unending uncertainty what the rules will be, who will make them, when they will come into effect, how long they will last, who may or may not fish, where, when, and how they may fish, and for what species they may fish. It is difficult to believe that we can achieve stable, sustainable fisheries if the system that is responsible for managing them is itself unstable and unpredictable. As the uncertainties, complexities, and litigation continue or increase, the premises and foundations of this structure ought to be critically reviewed.

Whatever the form of the management authority, however, whether the councils, a new commission, NMFS, or the courts, it will have to deal with the second category of problems and issues

- benign technologies, effective effort control, and an operational hypothesis of ecosystems management - that are inherent, fundamental, and unavoidable in mixed-species fisheries. These problems would require much greater effort of a different kind than that of reforming the structure of the management authority. We are persuaded that the council, or any other management entity, can only escape from a contentious, costly, and burdensome continuation of current management tactics if significant progress is made with the issues in the second category.

There can be little doubt that even with restored stocks, fishing pressure will continue at a high level, not just off New England but also around the world. If management is to be successful in sustaining fish resources under that heavy pressure at a reasonable cost and without waste, it must consider the closely interrelated issues inherent in traditional fishing technology, of effective control of fishing effort or fishing mortality, and of applying an operational concept of ecosystems management. We have said enough to make the case that controlling fishing mortality in single-species fisheries and especially in mixed-species fisheries with traditional fishing technologies, both on target species and on bycatch species, is very difficult if not impossible. This is particularly true in heavily exploited stocks where effort and mortality control is most important.

We argue that development of new concepts of benign and selective fishing technologies is desirable but will not by themselves be sufficient if management lacks the means of restraining effort and fishing mortalities. Managers must have access to strategies that can effectively restrain or limit effort and control fishing mortalities. The experience to date suggests that it does not have such strategies. Further, the hierarchical hypothesis of the structure and functions of ecosystems makes it clear that it is important to know *where* within fisheries systems control of fishing effort should be directed or applied, and where effort control may be less important or even unnecessary and management costs may thereby be reduced. The hypothesis tells us that the entire system may be destabilized if control of fishing mortality is misapplied or absent upon the stabilizing components of the system. The hypothesis tells us that effort control is particularly important on those components of the hierarchical system that lend constraints and stability to the dynamics of other components. Truly selective fishing gear with built-in limits on catch, such as we suggest is feasible, could be directed to where it is necessary to maintain the integrity and stability of the whole fisheries system. The hierarchical concept of ecosystems holds the potential for simplifying the management of multispecies fisheries and could accommodate the apparently inherent uncertainties of fisheries science.

We see little effort being made in any of these three areas of fundamental concern. It is true that experimental work is increasing in reducing some of the inherent limitations of the otter trawl. The improvements that have been achieved in reducing some bycatch species are encouraging, but the problems remain of scale damage, the rather crude selection among juveniles and adults as reflected in mesh selectivity data, and the impact of trawl doors upon some habitats. It is questionable that the trawl can become the truly selective and environmentally benign kind of gear that would be required to sustain fisheries at biomass levels required by present law that will continue to be subjected to substantial fishing pressure.

Some thought is being given to the problems that are evident in conventional effort control proposals. But the suggestions for corrections seem to be largely fine-tuning and small variations on traditional themes. The results seem to be increasing complexity of existing concepts and the probability of increasingly complicated rule-making. One of the clear lessons from the New England experience, and elsewhere, is that such trends increase the incentives and the opportunities for non-compliance. The whole problem of effective control on effort or on fishing mortality requires re-thinking, and, we believe, wholly new concepts - unless we were to develop harvesting gear such as we have suggested here that contains built-in and non-violable controls on fishing effort.

If there is no operational understanding of the nature of ecosystems, and if management does not recognize and manage those components of ecosystems that make sustainable fisheries possible, we believe management cannot succeed in sustaining fisheries. If fisheries ecosystems are so deranged by traditional fishing practices and by management strategies that lead to instability, then the variabilities of fish stocks can only increase, and the efficacy of management and management's predictive capabilities can only decrease. Success cannot be expected from unrealistically complicated and data-hungry concepts that would entail exorbitant costs and that would demand continual sticking of fingers in the dike. Success in this context depends upon identification and adoption of a working hypothesis of the nature of ecosystems that makes possible effective management within the realistic capabilities and resources of, and costs to management institutions. If our effort toward understanding the nature of ecosystems are to consist of "vague hand-waving," then we should indeed "brace ourselves for the collapse."

13) Abbreviations

ADF	Atlantic Demersal Finfish Plan
ASMFC	Atlantic States Marine Fisheries Commission
BRP	Biological Reference Point
CFN	*Commercial Fisheries News*
FAAS	Flexible Area Action System
FCZ	Fishery Conservation Zone
FMP	Fishery Management Plan
ICNAF	International Commission for Northwest Atlantic Fisheries
IP	Interim Plan
MFCMA	Magnuson Fishery Conservation and Management Act
MSY	Maximum Sustainable Yield
NEFMC	New England Fishery Management Council
NMFS	National Marine Fisheries Service
NOAA	National Oceanic and Atmospheric Administration
OSP	Optional Settlement Plan
OY	Optimum Yield
SAP	Special Access Program
SARC	Stock Assessment Review Committee
SAW	Stock Assessment Workshop
SFA	Sustainable Fisheries Act
TAC	Total Allowable Catch
TMG	Technical Monitoring Group

14) Glossary

Bycatch: Traditionally, the term bycatch has referred to species that account for less than fifty percent of the trip catch. MFCMA as amended defines bycatch as "fish which are harvested in a fishery, but which are not sold or kept for personal use, and includes economic discards and regulatory discards. Such term does not include fish released alive under a recreational catch and release fishery management program."

Demersal: pertaining to near or on the ocean bottom.

Discards: fish that may for a number of reasons be thrown away from a fishing vessel.

Exempted Fishery Program: a plan to permit the use of small-mesh otter trawls for unregulated species within regions of regulated species.

Fishing mortality: The amount or percent of fish that are killed by fishing activities rather than by natural causes.

High-grading: a practice of throwing away fish of lesser value so that only fish of higher value could be landed within a vessel trip limit or quota.

IFQ: Individual Fishing Quotas grant exclusive rights to a specific percent of a total allowable catch of a species, to an individual or corporation within a specific time and area. The holder of an IFQ may often buy or sell shares.

ITQ: Individual Transferable Quota. See IFQ.

Limited entry: Any one of a number of tactics by which the number and qualifications for entry of fishermen who may legally catch fish in general or a particular species of fish are controlled by regulation.

MSY: Maximum sustainable yield is the largest average annual catch or yield that can be taken over a significant period of time from each stock under prevailing ecological and environmental conditions.

Multispecies management: a somewhat vague concept of considering inter-relationships among species of fish in setting management regulations.

OY: Optimum Yield, as defined by MFCMA, "means the amount of fish (A) which will provide the greatest overall benefit to the Nation, with particular reference to food production and recreational opportunities; and (B) which is prescribed as such on the basis of the maximum sustainable yield from such fishery, as modified by any relevant economic, social, or ecological factor."

Optional Settlement Program: see Exempted Fisheries Program.

Otter trawl: a large net dragged on or near the ocean bottom. Large boards or "doors" are attached to each side of the mouth of the net in such a way that they spread apart and thus keep the mouth of the net open to catch fish.

Pulse fishing: a fishing strategy to achieve the greatest net income with the least costs.

Subsidization of ecosystems: any of a variety of methods whereby society attempts to replace natural functions of ecosystems that are lost due to natural or human perturbations; fish hatcheries, for example.

TAC: Total Allowable Catch is the total amount of fish that may be legally landed under the regulations of a management program.

15) References

Ahl, V. and T.F.H. Allen. 1996. *Hierarchy Theory: A Vision Vocabulary, and Epistemology*. New York: Columbia University Press.

Allen, T.F.H., J.A. Tainter, and T.W. Hoekstra. 2003. *Supply-side Sustainability*. New York: Columbia University Press.

Alverson, D.L. 1972. Science and fisheries management. In B.J. Rothschild, ed., *World Fisheries Policy*, 211-218. Seattle and London: University of Washington Press.

Alverson, D.L. 2002. Factors influencing the scope and quality of science and management decisions (The good, the bad and the ugly). Fish and Fisheries 3:3-19.

Alverson, D.L. 2004. Searching for ecosystem reality - terms and concepts. Bulletin of Marine Science 74:1-13.

Alverson, D.L., M.H. Freeberg, S.A. Murawski, and J.G. Pope. 1994. A global assessment of fisheries bycatch and discards. FAO Fisheries Technical Paper 339.

Anon. MS 1977. Assistance to determine management objectives. A report submitted to the New England Regional Fishery Management Council. Sagamore, MA., and Washington, D.C, Development Sciences Inc.

Anon. 2004. Bycatch in Northeast Fisheries: Moving Forward. Gloucester, MA. NOAA Fisheries Northeast Regional Office.

Anon. MS 2004. Individual Fishing Quotas: environmental, public trust, and socioeconomic impacts. Washington, D.C. The Marine Fish Conservation Network.

Apollonio, S. 2002. *Hierarchical Perspectives on Marine Complexities: Searching for Systems in the Gulf of Maine.* New York: Columbia University Press.

Auster, P.J. and N.L. Shackell. 1997. Fishery reserves. In J. Boreman, B.S. Nakashima, J.A. Wilson, and R.L. Kendall, eds. *Northwest Atlantic Groundfish: Perspectives on a Fishery Collapse,* 159-166. Bethesda, MD. American Fisheries Society.

Bean M.J. 1983. *The Evolution of National Wildlife Law.* New York: Praeger Publishers.

Bean, M.J., and M.J.Rowland. 1997. *The Evolution of National Wildlife Law.* 3rd Ed. New York: Praeger Publishers.

Bigelow, H.B. and W.C. Schroeder. 1953. *Fishes of the Gulf of Maine.* Fishery Bulletin of the Fish and Wildlife Service 74. Washington, D.C.: U.S. Government Printing Office.

Brodziak, J.K. T., P.M. Mace, W.J. Overholtz, and P.J. Rago. 2004. Ecosystem trade-offs in managing New England fisheries. Bulletin of Marine Science 74:529-548.

Carey, R.A. 1999. *Against the Tide: the Fate of New England Fishermen.* Boston: Houghton Mifflin Co.

Clover, C. 2006. *The End of the Line.* New York: The New Press.

Collette, B.B. and G. Klein-MacPhee. 2002. *Bigelow and Schroeder's Fishes of the Gulf of Maine.* 3rd Ed. Washington and London: Smithsonian Institution Press.

Commission on Marine Science, Engineering and Resources. 1969. *Our Nation and the Sea.* Washington D.C.: U.S. Government Printing Office.

Crockett, L. 2005. Improving the scientific basis for management by separating conservation and management decisions. In D. Witherell, ed. *Managing Our Nation's Fisheries II*, 190-6. Washington, D.C.: National Oceanic and Atmospheric Administration.

Dewar, M. 1983. *Industry in Trouble: The Federal Government and the New England Fisheries.* Philadelphia: Temple University Press.

Dobbs, D. 2000. *The Great Gulf: Fishermen, Scientists, and the Struggle to Revive the World's Greatest Fishery.* Washington, D.C. Island Press/Shearwater Books.

Doeringer, P.B., P.L. Moss, and D.G. Terkla. 1986. *The New England Fishing Economy: Jobs, Income, and Kinship.* Amherst, MA.: The University of Massachusetts Press.

Ellis, R. 2003. *The Empty Ocean.* Washington, D.C.: Shearwater.

Fogarty, M. n.d. Ecology of the Northeast Continental Shelf: Toward an Ecosystem Approach to Fisheries Management. Northeast Fisheries Science Center and Northeast Regional Office, National Marine Fisheries service.

Food and Agriculture Organization (FAO). 1997a. The State of World Fisheries and Aquaculture. 1996. Rome: Food and Agriculture Organization of the United Nations.

Food and Agriculture Organization (FAO). 1997b. Commodity Market Review 1996-97. Rome: Food and Agriculture Organization of the United Nations.

Fordham, S.V. 1996. New England Groundfish: from Glory to Grief. A Portrait of America's Most Devastated Fishery. Washington, D.C. Center for Marine Conservation.

Gavaris, S. 1993. Analytical estimates of reliability for the projected yield from commercial fisheries. p. 185-191. In S.J. Smith, J.J. Hunt, and D. Rivard, eds. Risk evaluation and biological reference points for fisheries management. Can. Spec. Publ. Fish. Aquat. Sci. 120.

Gislason, H., M. Sinclair, K. Sainsbury, and R. O'Boyle. 2000. Symposium overview: incorporating ecosystem objectives within fisheries management. ICES Journal of Marine Science. 57: 468-475.

Gulland, J.A. 1969. *Manual of Methods for Fish Stock Assessment. Part 1. Fish Population Analysis.* F.A.O. Manuals in Fisheries Science 4.

Gulland, J.A. 1971. Science and fishery management. Journal du Conseil 33(3):471-7.

Gulland, J.A. 1972. *The Fish Resources of the Ocean.* London: Fishing News Books, Ltd.

Gulland, J.A. 1974. *The Management of Marine Fisheries.* Seattle: University of Washington Press.

Halliday, R.G. and A.T. Pinhorn. 1997. Policy Frameworks. In J. Boreman, B.S. Nakashima, J.A. Wilson, and R.L. Kendall, eds. *Northwest Atlantic Groundfish: Perspectives on a Fishery Collapse,* 95-109. Bethesda, MD. American Fisheries Society.

Hennemuth, R.C., B.J. Rothschild, L.G. Anderson, and W.A Lund, Jr. 1980. Overview document of the northeast fishery management task force, Phase 1. NOAA Technical Memorandum NMFS-F/NEC-1. Woods Hole, MA.: Northeast Fisheries Center

Hennessey, T. and M. Healey. 2000. Ludwig's ratchet and the collapse of New England groundfish stocks. Coastal Management 28:187-213.

Hilborn, R. 2003. The state of the art in stock assessment: where are we and where are we going. Scientia Marina 67: 15-20.

Hilborn, R., A.E. Punt, and J. Orensanz. 2004. Beyond band-aids in fisheries management: fixing world fisheries. Bulletin of Marine Science 74(3):493-507.

Hilborn, R. and J.Valero. 2004. An assessment of the scientific advice on the status of New England herring stocks. Report submitted to the New England Fishery Management Council.

Hutchinson, G.E. 1948. Circular causal systems in ecology. Annals of the New York Academy of Sciences 50:221-246.

Kurien, J. 1998. Traditional ecological knowledge and ecosystem sustainability: On giving new meaning to Asian coastal proverbs. Ecological Applications 8(1) Supplement:S2-S5.

Larkin, P. A. 1972. A confidential memorandum on fisheries science. In B.J. Rothschild, ed., *World Fishing Policy*, 189-197. Seattle and London: University of Washington Press.

Larkin. P.A. 1977. An epitaph for the concept of maximum sustained yield. Transactions of the American Fisheries Society 106:1-11.

Larkin, P.A. 1980. Objectives of management. In R.T. Lackey and L.A. Nielsen, eds. *Fisheries Management*, 245-262. New York and Toronto: John Wiley and Sons.

Link, J.S. 2002. What does ecosystem-based fisheries management mean? Fisheries 27(4):18-21.

Mann, K.H. 1982. *Ecology of Coastal Waters: A Systems Approach.* Oxford: Blackwell.

McGlade, J. 1999. Bridging disciplines: the role of scientific advice, especially biological modeling. In J. Kooiman, M. Van Vliet, and S. Jentoft, eds., *Creative Governance: Opportunities for Fisheries in Europe,* 75-185. Aldershot, U.K.: Ashgate.

National Research Council. 1998. Review of northeast fishery stock assessments. Washington, D.C.: National Academy Press.

National Research Council. 1999. *Sustaining Marine Fisheries.* Washington, D.C.: National Academy Press.

O'Neill, R.V., D.L. DeAngelis, J.B. Waide, and T.F.H. Allen, 1986. *A Hierarchical Concept of Ecosystems.* Princeton, N.J.: Princeton University Press.

Overholtz, W.J. 1985. Managing the multispecies otter trawl fisheries of Georges Bank with catch optimization methods. North American Journal of Fisheries Management 5:252-260.

Pattee, H.H. 1972. The evolution of self-simplifying systems. In E. Lazlo, ed., *The Relevance of General Systems Theory,* 31-41. New York: Brazillier.

Pattee, H.H. 1973. The physical basis and origin of hierarchical control. in H.H. Pattee, ed. *Hierarchy Theory: the Challenge of Complex Systems,* 73-107. New York: George Brazilier.

Pattee, H.H. 1978. The complementarity principle in biological and social structures. Journal of Social and Biological Structures 1:191-200.

Pauly, D., and J. MacLean. 2003. *In a Perfect Ocean.* Washington, Covelo, London: Island Press.

Pierce, D.E. MS 1982. Development and evolution of fisheries management plans for cod, haddock, and yellowtail flounder. New England Fishery Management Council.

Playfair, S.R. 2003. *Vanishing Species.* Hanover and London: University Press of New England.

Popper, K. R. 1990. *A World of Propensities.* Bristol: Thoemmes.

Rieser, A. 1999. Prescriptions for the commons: environmental scholarship and the fishing quotas debate. Harvard Environmental Law Review 23(2):393-421.

Root, R.B. 1967. The niche exploitation pattern of the blue-gray gnatcatcher. Ecological Monographs 37:317-50.

Rose, G.A. 1993. Cod spawning on a migration highway in the northwest Atlantic. Nature 366:458-61.

Rose, G.A. 1997. The trouble with fisheries science! Reviews in Fish Biology and Fisheries 7:365-370.

Rothschild, B.J., R.C. Hennemuth, J.J. Dykstra, L.C. Murphy, Jr., J.C. Bryson, and J.D. Ackert. 1980. Methodology for identification and analysis of fishery management options. NOAA Technical Memorandum NMFS-F-7. Woods Hole, MA.: Northeast Fisheries Center.

Rothschild, B., C. Clark, R. Hennemuth, R. Lasker, M. Sissenwine, W. Wooster, and J. Steele. MS 1982. Report of the Fisheries Ecology Meeting June 8-11, 1981. Woods Hole Oceanographic Institution WHOI-82-28.

Rothschild, B.J., A.F. Sharov, and M. Lambert. 1997. Single-species and multispecies management. In J. Boreman, B.S. Nakashima, J.A. Wilson, and R.L. Kendall, eds. *Northwest Atlantic Groundfish: Perspectives on a Fishery Collapse,* 141-152 Bethesda, MD.: American Fisheries Society.

Safina, C. 1997. *Song for a Blue Ocean.* New York: Henry Holt and Company

Shelley, P., J. Atkinson, E. Dorsey, P. Brooks. 1996. The New England Fisheries crisis: what have we learned? Tulane Law Journal 9:221-244.

Sinclair, A.F. and S.A. Murawski. 1997. Why have groundfish stocks declined? In J.Boreman, B.S. Nakashima, J.A. Wilson, and R.L. Kendall, eds., *Northwest Atlantic Groundfish: Perspectives on a Fishery Collapse*, 71-93. Bethesda, MD.: American Fisheries Society.

Sissenwine, M.P. 1984. Why do fish populations vary? In R.M. May, ed., *Exploitation of Marine Communities*. 59-94. New York: Springer-Verlag.

Sissenwine, M.P., and A.A. Rosenberg. 1993, Marine fisheries at a critical juncture. Fisheries 18:6-13.

Steele, J.H. 1980. Patterns in plankton. Oceanus 23(2):3-8.

Thorson, G. 1971. *Life in the Sea.* New York, Toronto: McGraw-Hill Book Company.

Townsend, R.E. and A.T. Charles. 1997. User rights in fishing. 1997.In J. Boreman, B.S. Nakashima, J.A. Wilson, and R.L. Kendall, eds., *Northwest Atlantic Groundfish: Perspectives on a Fishery Collapse*, 177-184. Bethesda, MD.: American Fisheries Society.

Ulanowicz, R.E. 1997. *Ecology: the Ascendent Perspective.* New York: Columbia University Press.

U.S. Department of Commerce. 1976. A marine fisheries program for the nation. Washington, D.C. Government Printing Office.

Walters, C., and J-J. Maguire. 1996. Lessons for stock assessment from the northern cod collapse. Reviews in Fish Biology and Fisheries 6(2):125-138.

Weber, M.L. 2002. *From Abundance to Scarcity: a History of U.S. Marine Fisheries Policy.* Washington, Covelo, London: Island Press.

Woodward, C. 2004. *The Lobster Coast.* New York: Viking.

16) Appendix

NEW ENGLAND REGIONAL FISHERY MANAGEMENT COUNCIL

Groundfish Committee
February 27-28, 1978
Recommendations

1. A vessel shall have on board nets of the appropriate and specified mesh size whenever 20% of the weight of all fish on board is of a regulated species or when 20% of the weight of all fish on board are regulated species (2 or more species).

2. A vessel with 20% by weight of all fish on board of a regulated species, or 20% by weight of all fish on board of the aggregate of regulated species shall have on board only nets of a mesh size no smaller than the mesh size specified for those regulated species.

3. Section 651.4(b) which specifies that the masters of vessels shall ensure compliance of all persons on board with fisheries regulations shall be referred to NOAA/NMFS for review of the legal responsibilities of master, crew, and passengers on vessels carrying passengers for hire.

4. The yellowtail flounder fishery east of 69E W. Long. shall be an incidental catch fishery only.

5. Suggested quarterly allocations for yellowtail flounder east of 69E W. Long. shall be as follows: (1) reserved, (2) 950 MT, (3) 1150 MT, (4) 800 MT.

17) Index